The Village to Village Guide for Pilgrims walking the Camino Santiago

2nd Edition
Revised & Updated

Jaffa Raza

© 2007 Simon Wallenberg ISBN 1-84356-001-1
       Second Edition

   First Edition Published 2001

All rights reserved. Printed in the United Kingdom. No part of this book may be used or reproduced in any form or by any means, or stored in a database or retrieval system, without prior written permission of the publisher except in the case of brief quotations embodied in critical articles and reviews.

British Library Catalog Number:

Published by The Simon Wallenberg Press

Printed in the United Kingdom

Warning and Disclaimer
This book is sold as is, without warranty of any kind, either express or implied. While every precaution has been taken in the preparation of this book, the authors and Simon Wallenberg Press assume no responsibility for errors or omissions. Neither is any liability assumed for damages resulting from the use of the information or instructions contained herein. It is further stated that the publisher and authors are not responsible for any damage or loss that results directly or indirectly from your use of this book.

Jaffa Raza

The Village to Village Guide for Pilgrims walking the Camino Santiago

Reconstruction of the Abbey of Cluny

Simon Wallenberg Press

The Route covered by the Village to Village Guide from St Jean Pied Du Port to Santiago

Distances between villages/towns in Kilometers

St. Jean Pied de Port 27
Roncesvalles 19
Zubri 21
Pamplona 24
Sanguesa 26
Puente la Reina 19
 Estella
19
Los Arcos 18
Vianna 8
Logrono 10
Navarrete 15
Najera 6
Azofra
14   San Domingo Calzada
6
Granon
16
Belorado 11
Villafranca Montez deOca 11
San Juan de Ortega 26
Burgos 19
Hornillos del Camino 21
Hontanas 7
Castrojeriz 10
Itero de la Vega 12
Fromista 14
Villalcazar de Sirga 6

Carrion de los Condez 22
Calzadilla de la Cueza 20
Shagun
18
Burgo Raneo 19
Mansilla de las Mulas 16
Leon 6
Vigen del Camino 23
Hospital de Orbigo 18
Astorga 21
Rabanal del Camino 5
Cruz de Ferro 18
Molinaseca 6
Ponferrada 13
Cacabelos 8
Villafranca del Bierzo 15
Vega de Valcarce 11
O Cebreiro 23
Triacasdtela 10
Samos 8
Sarria 18
Portomarin 28
Palas do Rei 14
Melide 14
Arzua 26
Lavacolla 10
Santiago de Compostela

In the beginning of the IX Century, when the Moslem invasion was practically consolidated and only the kingdoms of the North resisted its domination. A figure was needed that could unify the fight against the common enemy and could, at the same time, serve as moral support to this important historic activity.

During the battles, if the Moors called on Mohammed, the Christians called on Saint James.

In this way that humble Saint, friend of the poor, who believed in the power of the word, became a warrior "-Santiago Matamoros (killer of Moors)" .

Since that moment, he presided over the most important battles of the Re-Conquest and the Christians, little by little, recovered their domains and converted Compostela into the principal centre of spiritual attraction of the Asturian-Leonese kingdom.

Santiago eventually competed with Rome and Jerusalem in power of attraction, becoming the largest centre of pilgrimage in the whole of Christaindom.

St James the Moor Slayer

Dedication

ElIas Valiña Sampedro (1929-1989), parish priest of Cebreiro and Doctor of Canon Law of the University of Salamanca. Scholar and an expert on Compostelan studies, he was awarded the 'Antonia de Nebrija' Prize (1967) for his thesis 'El Camino de Santiago, Estudio histórico-juridico' (Madrid 1971) and the 'José Maria Cuadrado' Prize (1986) for the 'Catdlogo de los archivos parroquiales de Ia diócesis de Lugo'(Lugo 1991).
In 1984 he began the marking of the Camino with yellow arrows from the French border to Santiago de Compostela and dedicated his efforts to the revitalisation of the Jacobean routes and to the promotion of the Asociaciones de Amigos, activities which culminated in the first International Congress at Jaca (1987).

Upon his tomb, in the pre-romanesque church of Santa Maria la Real at Cebreiro, his epitaph reads:
VIAE SANCTI JACOBI INSIGNIS RESTAURATOR
ET OMNIUM PEREGRINORUM AMICUS ET FRATER
(He was distinguished for his renovation of the Way of St. James and was friend and brother to all pilgrims).

Introduction

The pilgrims in the middle Ages believed that certain places and certain objects possessed unusual spiritual powers and that these sacred objects consecrated whatever came within their immediate environment. These objects or relics were believed to have miracalous properties.
The vast majority of pilgrims to Santiago undertook the long and hazardous journey, far from home, from a spirit of piety. Their piety was a form of after life insurance against the promise of eternal damnation.
A mediaeval church obsessed by the imminence of the Second Coming and the Day of Judgment promised eternal damnation relentlessly from the pulpit, and it was preached no less eloquently by the sculptors and painters who decorated the churches in which those sermons were heard.
This was the cause of the mediaeval cult of holy relics and the pre-eminence of the three pilgrimages in the middle Ages. The one to Jerusalem, that to Rome, and the one to Santiago de Compostela and the tomb of St James the Apostle.
Santiago became the most popular object of pilgrimage of the three, in the later middle Ages, and engendered an intensity of devotion that was maintained over the entire period of the growth of Christianity and Christian art in Europe, from the 10th to the 18th century.
Throughout those centuries the route to Santiago became a principal high road of Christian teaching, Christian institutions and Christian art.

The Celtic legend about the footpath

Santiago, far away under the mists and Atlantic skies of Galicia, all woods and water in a Celtic landscape of menhirs and lost gods, had always exerted an appeal that was infinitely pre Christian.
The pilgrim journeyed in order to pay the prescribed respect, out of duty, out of love, out of fear or out of a drive towards self improvement or superiority. However since these relics consisted of the earthly remains of sacred figures, there was an overlapping

with pre Christian Celtic beliefs, the cult of the dead, widespread in Europe since pre historic times.

The same path was a Roman trade-route, nicknamed by travellers la voje ladee, the Milky Way the road under the stars. The pale arm of the Milky Way stretched out and pointed the way to the edge of the known world where the sun went down: to Cape Finisterre (from the Latin firns terra-the end of the earth).

It was here that Roman legionary Decimo July Brutus, saw the Sun being extinguished in the waters of the ocean every evening. He insisted that when this happened there was a hissing sound similar to the one iron makes when it is tempered in the forge.

The iconography of the pilgrim route have led some to speculate on the meaning of the floral motif that recurs in mediaeval churches all along the way, as to whether it might, in origin, be not a flower, but a sun image of Celtic origin from our dim past.

We know that for pilgrims reaching Santiago in the Middle Ages it was obligatory to venture on to the chapel of Nuestra Senora at Finisterre, the last finger of land crooked into the ocean. One explanation for this is that there may have been a earlier journey to heaven, more mystical and of far earlier provenance than the church could have expected to acknowledge. The myth then must go back to earlier times and that the first pilgrims may have travelled the Camino to Cap Fimsterre even before the birth of Christ, going as supplicants to some forgotten god. Legend has it that the Druids the priestly caste of the Celtic people worshipped father Dis, who lived at the end of the world.

The modern day legend

Even though some people maintain that walking the route to Finis Terrae was part of the rites of the "Ancient Religion" the modern day legend started with burial of St James the Elder who identified with the doctrine of Christ and became the principal leader of the community of believers in Jerusalem.

James was admired for the fervor and sincerity of his preaching. It is believed that he first made the journey from Palestine to

Spain in a trading ship. Landing in Andalusia, he began to preach. He continued his evangelistic mission in Coimbra and Braga and then, passed to Iria Flavia in the Spanish Finisterre, where he would begin evangelization by frequenting places of pagan worship. James then returned to Palestine and formed the basic unit of the Primitive Church of Jerusalem, with the group of "Twelve", playing an outstanding role in the Christian community of the Holy City.

James then returned home to Jerusalem and some time later Herod Agripa, King of Judea, in order to please the Jews and to give a lesson to the Christian community, sentenced James to death by beheading.

The "miraculous arrival" of the corpse of the Apostle Saint James to Spain is the origin of the pilgrimage we know today. The legend says that his disciples stole their master's corpse and put it on board a ship without a crew. After seven days the ship arrived at the mouth of the River Ulla in Galicia. After a series of miraculous happenings, the Apostle was buried in the place that would later become the town of Santiago.

In the ninth century Pelagius, a hermit living in that part of Spain, had a vision (which he subsequently reported to Theodomir, bishop of Ira Flavia) in which he saw a very large bright star, surrounded by a ring of smaller ones, shining over a deserted spot in the hills. The matter was investigated and a tomb was found there containing three bodies.

They were identified as those of Saint James and two of his followers and when Alfonso II, King of the Asturias (791-824), went there he declared Saint James the patron saint of Spain. He built a church and a small monastery over the tomb in the saint's honor, around which a town grew up. It was known as campus de Ia stella or campus steliae later shortened to compostela. This is one explanation of the origin of the name. Another is that it derives from the Latin componere (to bury), as a Roman cemetery or early Christian necropolis is known to have existed under the site of the present day cathedral in Santiago - and where the remains of Saint James are still believed to be housed.

News of the discovery soon spread. It was encouraged to do so, moreover, both by Archbishop Gelmirez and the cathedral authorities, who were anxious to promote the town as a pilgrimage centre, thus attracting money to the area, and by the monks of the powerful Cluniac Order who were the principal promoters of pilgrimages in the Middle Ages. The monks of Cluny, saw in it the opportunity to assist the Spanish church in their long struggle against the Moors. Moreover the Turks had seized the Holy Sepulcher in 1078, thus putting a stop to pilgrimages to Jerusalem.

Among the stream of pilgrims that the centuries have seen on the route, are monarchs, church princes, noblemen, adventurers and beggars of all descriptions, including rogues and scoundrels such as Don Diego de Torres Villaroel, as well as old Christians steeped in simple faith, innocent multitudes moved by the Compostela miracle, troubadours... pilgrims all. We can see them in the inns and hospices where many have left traces of their passing (and sometimes their bones). Above all, we can see them reverberating through their written accounts where they have left their fatigue and their faith.

Among the thousands of devotees of St. James who went to Santiago by the Northern Way, throughout the centuries, the figure of St. Francis of Assisi particularly stands out. According to tradition, he travelled to San Salvador de Oviedo and to Santiago de Compostela in 1214.

The footpath to Santiago

Long-distance footpaths avoid not only large towns but even quite small villages as well; the Way of Saint James, on the other hand, because of its historic origins and the need for shelter, deliberately seeks them out. The footpath created since the very beginning an extraordinary spiritual, cultural and economical vitality: it bred literature, music, art and history and, on its account, cities and villages were born, hospitals and lodgings were built, commercial ways and new markets appeared, new roads and bridges were planned and cathedrals and churches, that elevated the Romanesque art to a magnificence not reached by other styles, were built.

Its 800 kilometers from the Saint Jean Pied de Port in the foothills of the Pyrenees to Santiago de Compostela in the western reaches of Galicia have changed little. Sections of it have now become modern roads and many of the "hospitals" and other accommodation set-up by religious orders along the way have long since disappeared, the Camino, still passes through the same villages, crosses the same rivers, visits the same chapels, churches, cathedrals and other monuments as did the path taken when the numbers walking peaked in the eleventh and twelfth centuries. It was at this time when over half a million people a year are said to have made the pilgrimage from different parts of Europe.

The pilgrimage today

Today several thousand people walk the Way every year, whether from the Pyrenees, from different parts of France or from even further afield: it is not uncommon, even nowadays, to meet Swiss, German, Belgian or Dutch pilgrims, for example, who have set out from home to make the entire journey on foot. Most parts of the walker's route are also accessible to those riding mountain (though not touring) bikes.
The walk takes about a month and there are a number of refuges set up to accommodate the genuine pilgrim and not the tourist. Some of these are in old monasteries, inns and seminaries others are provided by the villages along the way. Some are in grand establishments like the old Augustine abbey of Roncesvalles in the Pyrenees or the 12-centaury seminary at Puerto Reina

The Body of St James arrives in Spain

Practical advice for planning your journey

When to Go:
The normal pilgrim season is from March to October, but seems to be getting longer, partly due to high season pressures. Pilgrims, traditionally, wanted to arrive in Santiago a day or two before the feast of St. James on the 25th of July. This is a memorable time as the city is in fiesta for several days. In the last few years there has been an increase in demand on the facilities along the way, especially the nearer you get to Santiago. This problem is most acute during the two weeks leading up to the 25th of July when the whole route is crowded with pilgrims. It is difficult to get accommodation and a quiet night's rest. August is also a busy month and there may be water shortages along the way. Pilgrims traveling at this time of the year are advised to avoid the refuges in the larger towns, carry tents or use the hotels. If you travel during mid September to end October or mid April to June bad weather risks increase in the mountains, you will miss the major fiesta but accommodation, whether in refuge or hotel, will be easier to find. This guide book recommends these cooler and less crowded months as the best time to go.

Planning Your Journey:
Plan your journey according to the amount of time available to you. Those who can get away from their jobs for a short time will not be able to walk more than 1200 km. in one trip. If this is the case you will have to make your pilgrimage in several stages of say two weeks at a time. You will need to walk a minimum of 100 km. or cycle a minimum of 200 km. to qualify for the traditional certificate of pilgrimage or compostela. granted by the Santiago cathedral authorities.

In France the starting points are Vezelay, Le Puy or Arles. Jean-Pied-de-Port, on the other side of the Pyrenees from Spain is the most popular starting point in France. In Spain, the starting points are from Roncesvalles at the top of the Pyrenees above St. Jean or from any one of the cities along the route: Pamplona, Burgos, Leon, Astorga or Ponferrada.

Time Taken For The Pilgrimage.

The distance between St-Jean-Pied-de-Port on the French side of the Pyrenees and Santiago is approximately 800 kilometres. .Walkers, depending on their pace, stamina and desire to have some rest days, generally allow between four and six weeks, while cyclists will need around two weeks on average..

Pilgrims Passport or 'Credential del peregrino' is essential if you wish to stay in the Refugios.

The Abbey at Roncevalles will give you a Pilgrims Passport. At the start of your journey apply to the Abbots office. If you get this document stamped (with the 'sello' or rubber stamp) at monasteries, churches, town halls ('ayuntamientos') or other establishments along the way, it will serve as proof of your pilgrimage and help you obtain a 'compostela' or certificate of pilgrimage when you arrive at the Cathedral in Santiago . The record has to be shown at refuges if you wish to obtain accommodation.

The pilgrim record is known as the 'credential del peregrino' and is available in a number of places in Spain, and in pilgrim refuges. 2001 pilgrims who wish to stay in the refuges along the way and to obtain their 'compostela' in Santiago are recommended to carry the Spanish 'credential' . There should be no trouble in getting both documents stamped as described above. It may be helpful to have a letter of introduction from your parish, college or similar organization to present when requesting a credencial although this is not always required.

Maps and Guidebooks:

Whatever mode of transport you use, good maps are essential and a detailed guidebook (especially for walkers) may also be helpful. If you have been following the GR65 (Le Puy to Roncesvalles) in France you will find nothing to compare with the French 'topo guides'. All the commercially-2-available maps are inadequate mainly because of the amount of road-building that has taken place in northern Spain, particularly Galicia, in recent years.

The Michelin maps 441 and 442 are excellent maps and may be obtained from Telegraph Online at www.telegraph.com

Preparing for the Journey:

For the not so experienced long distance walkers and cyclists careful preparation and training will make a big difference to the travelers comfort on the camino. Walking boots or shoes will have to be tried and tested. Trainers are not adequate in bad weather, particularly the winter months. For sore or 'hot' spots that can develop on feet, animal wool available from chemists, provides excellent padding. Dr Scholl's adhesive foam is also effective. Clean socks (wool/cotton looped variety) each day also makes a big difference.

You could consider joining a local rambling club and go for weekend walks, starting with slower, shorter ones, and gradually build up speed and stamina. If buying a rucksack for the first time, try on several and get the one that fits you most comfortably. When out walking wear your rucksack and increase its weight gradually until you are carrying all your equipment. Fill your rucksack only with absolutely essential items and the total weight of it should not be more than ten per cent of your body weight. This will include water and provisions for the day. If you plan to sleep in pilgrim refuges you will need a light-weight sleeping bag, with a sleeping mat and a small torch. Ear-plugs and lip-salve are also useful.

Take along a first aid kit with basic necessities which include bandage, plasters, antiseptic cream, iodine, anti-inflammatory cream for sore and tired joints, asprin, diarrhoea tablets and Compeed to apply over blistered areas. Apply Vaseline in areas prone to blisters prior to walking.

Finally you need to be prepared for continuing and torrential rain, especially in Galicia, and for the problem of never really getting dry. Keeping dry clothes (and money etc.) in plastic bags is a great help. Cyclists with 27" (touring) wheels will find inner tubes scarce and tyres non-existent so you may wish to bring spares. A 2000 cyclist found cycle repair shops in the smaller places better stocked and more pilgrim orientated (eg Sahagun, Villafranca delBierzo) than the larger cities. Spares are more readily available for bikes with 26 and 28" tyres.

Language:

A basic knowledge of Spanish, via evening classes or home-study tapes, will add enormously to your enjoyment. English is not spoken in rural Spain and is rarely spoken in towns, even in tourist offices. Expect to have to communicate in Spanish all the time and you will be surprised at the progress you make. Take a small dictionary with you or buy one in a town bookshop. Once you reach Galicia you may find that people answer you in Galician ('gallego') which is related to Portuguese.

Getting to Spain by land, air or sea.

If departing from England Rynair serves the entire region via flights to Puy, Santiago de Compestela, Biarritz and Santander. Flights if booked well in advance can be purchased at very low cost.

Ryanair to Biarritz. There is an airport bus to Bayonne railway station from where there are trains to Saint-Jean-Pied-de-Port. See www.voyages-sncf.com for up to date timetables and fares.

Ryanair to Valladolid. There are bus connections to Leon. See www.alsa.es for details. Ryanair to Santander. EasyJet to Bilbao. Take the airport bus to city centre 18 mins 1.50€. Or else take the metro service from Sondiko station.

The Tourist Office at the airport is open until 2300, From Bilbao to Saint-Jean: Coach service to Hendaye. Tickets and bus stop at Termibus by the Hospital Civil de Basuto. 1 hr 55mins. 7.50€. Hendaye by train to Saint Jean via Bayonne is three and a half hours. From Bilbao to Pamplona, Roncesvalles or Saint-Jean. Coach service 5 times a day to Pamplona. Local bus service from there to Roncesvalles, run by a comapny called Autocares Artieda,

The route in this guide starts just before the French/Spanish border and assumes that pilgrims will have reached the French border town of St-Jean-Pied-de-Port, possibly using one of the three routes across France (from Paris/Tours, Vezelay or Le Puy) that meet near Ostabat. There is a direct train service from Bayonne to St Jean five times a day.

The first two trains, the 9.28 and the 11.28, took bikes in 2000. Bayonne can be reached by train from Paris or by coach from London: Eurolines have a London to Bayonne service at a cost of around £125 return. Bilbao has direct air services from London via EasyJet the low cost aurline and, if using Iberia, it is possible to return from Santiago. Bicycles are carried free of charge within normal weight limits.

From Bilbao there is a frequent coach service to Hendaye (tickets and stop in the Plaza Arrezola). From Hendaye take the train via Bayonne to St. Jean, three hours. Cyclists are recommended to cycle to Cambo-les-Bains and pick up one of the two morning trains to St Jean.
For those starting their journey from Pamplona, there is a coach service from Bilbao five times a day. Bikes are sometimes allowed on the coaches.One can also fly to Pamplona via Barcelona or Madrid.
Direct trains go from Bilbao to Logrono and Burgos on the route. Duration of journey is three hours and tickets cost 18 Euros. Buses from Bilbao are run by ALSA in calle Autonomica. One and a half hours and 1435 ptas to Logrono and two hours to Burgos. If you stay overnight in Bilbao the calle Bidebarrita has several hotels and is convenient for the station on the other side of the river. The cathedral at Bilbao is dedicated to St James and has a modern statue of him. Now that it is no longer possible to send bicycles registered from Victoria Station to France, an alternative way for cyclists to reach St Jean is to fly (on a cheap charter) to Lourdes.

This worked very well for a 2000 pilgrim who used St Peter's Pilgrims, telephone (081)-698 3788. If you prefer to travel by sea, there is a direct service, operating twice a week by P &

O Ferries from Portsmouth. 15 km. from the city center is the ferry port of Santurzi. There is a FEVE train and a number of coaches to the center.

From Plymouth to Santander one can travel by Britanny Ferries. From near the ferry port The Auto coach goes to Burgos. Three hours and the cost is 20 Euros. Alsa coach goes every night to Pamplona. Duration of journey four hours. Cost 25 Euros. Alsa bus leaves every night for Leon. Cost of journey 30 Euros.

For timetables of Spanish railways and of bus companies go to www.renfe.es, www.alsa.es and www.continental-auto.es. The ferry companies are at www.brittanyferries.com and www.poferries.com.

Money:
ATMs in all towns and large villages. Debit cards can also be used as a VISA card. ATMs give a choice of language. If outside bank hours they appear to be in a locked lobby area there will be, somewhere on the door, a place to 'swipe' your card and so get in. They accept most cards look for the 'Cirrus' logo and use your normal cash card. You are not restricted to using the machines in any particular bank. The two main signs to look for are Telebanco and SeiviRed. They have distinctive logos that you will soon learn to spot at 100 metres. The normal withdrawal limit is 150€ per day

Internet Access:
Many refugios now have internet. However there are a lot of pilgrims contending for use, and they are usually Windows 98, and the usb ports and/or cd drives may not be available. There are also internet cafes in the larger towns, as well as in the library. Uploading photos can be a problem.

Health Care:
Cruz Roja (Red Cross) centers provide free emergency care for pilgrims. Refugio hosts and other pilgrims will give you help and

advice on caring for blisters and other typical walker's problems. Check to see if your current health coverage needs anything special to cover major medical emergencies while traveling in Spain.

Accommodation:
Staying in smaller towns or villages is often much more enjoyable than searching for accommodation in the big cities.
If you do decide to stay in e.g. Pamplona, Logrono, Burgos or Leon, try to avoid arriving in the early evening rush-hour between 6 and 8pm when roads and pavements are crowded and hotel rooms possibly already taken, especially at weekends and fiesta times.
Accommodation along the camino ranges from luxury hotels like the state-run paradors to very basic pilgrim refuges ('refugios'). The word 'hotel' generally indicates a higher standard of comfort (at a price) than 'hostal', which in turn implies more comfort and facilities than a 'fonda' and, going down the scale, a 'posada'. Most hostals and fondas provide acceptable accommodation at a reasonable price. A number of bars in Spain also have rooms, sometimes elsewhere in the village or town.
Even if a bar is full or has no rooms, they may know somewhere else to try or know a neighbour who will put pilgrims up in their home ('casa privada'). It is also worthwhile asking at restaurants. The word 'habitaciones' means 'rooms' and 'camas' 'beds'. If you want to leave early in the morning, you should arrange to pay the night before and ask to be shown how the exterior locks work. Otherwise, you may have to wait until well after 9am.

Refuges:
Pilgrim refuges (or 'refugios') exist in many towns and villages, provided by monasteries, the parish, the town hall, the regional Amigos del Camino de Santiago or by individuals who enjoy meeting pilgrims.

A number of new refuges were built last year, particularly in Galicia where there should be refuges every 10 to 15 kilometres. It is not known if they will all have wardens in 2001 or be open early and late in the season. Facilities in the refuges vary considerably: sometimes only floorspace is available, while other refuges have bunk beds or mattresses.

A sleeping bag is essential, a sleeping mat advisable, an inflatable pillow and plug for basin useful. Refuges described in this guide as 'basic' will have floorspace for sleeping bags, electric light, a cold water tap and a w.c. Other facilities, where known, will be mentioned, e.g. shower, kitchen(with or without pans etc.), bunk beds, hot water, drying facilities etc. In July and August there may well be serious water shortages in certain places on the camino when the supply will be turned off for up to 12 hours at a time.

Please be sparing in your use of water. You will probably be asked by the voluntary warden ('hospitalero') to show your pilgrim record (and/or 'credencial')before being admitted as the refuges are intended for true pilgrims, on foot or travelling by bicycle, not just holiday-makers. Nor are they intended for small or large groups with back-up transport or for motorists. Despite this, in busy months you may still encounter large groups with their attendant disadvantages. Some refuges, including the Refugio Gaucelmo at Rabanal, do not accept large groups and do not accept bookings made in advance by leaders who arrive early with a vehicle.

At busy times preference is also given to walkers over cyclists, simply because it is easier for a cyclist to go on to the next refuge. However each refuge, with or without full-time wardens, has its own house rules, or lack of them. Some refuges charge a small set fee of 150 to 500 pesetas, others request a voluntary donation while others still make no charge. The doors of most refuges are locked 11pm and pilgrims encouraged to be away by 8am.

Camping:

Prices at campsites have risen considerably over recent years. Some charge the motorcycle fee for bicycles, so that two people with bikes can pay more than if they arrived in a car. Some class I sites charge 2000 pesetas plus for two people, two bikes and one small tent, although the average was around 1000.

Sites are nearly all crowded (and noisy) in July and August. Opening times and facilities are listed for campsites.

Security:

It is sensible, particularly in towns and cities, to establish your accommodation first, and lock up your bike and bags before going sightseeing. If possible lock your bike to a solid fixture in the garage or lock-up place and, of course, if you have to leave it in the street. For personal valuables an old-fashioned, out-of-sight money-belt may be safer than the modern, more visible versions. Don't assume that you can leave anything safely outside in towns, even in quiet places; sad but true all over Europe.

Road safety:

Lorries and cars are usually considerate of cyclists. Times to take particular care are when starting off (keep to the right) and late afternoon when you and drivers behind you will be travelling into the sun. Walkers should walk on the left of the road facing oncoming traffic. 'Camino' safety is also an issue and cyclists on mountain bikes should respect the rights of walkers on narrow paths.

Dealing with dogs:

Spanish dogs are less of a problem than French ones but can occasionally be troublesome. Walkers will find a stick useful for a number of reasons, including keeping a dog at bay. Keep away from sheep and cattle being guarded by dogs and don't turn your back on dogs until at a safe distance. Avoiding eye contact is another tip. It is possible to buy a special alarm that emits a high-pitched noise that is supposed to stop a dog in its tracks; the cost is around £30. The word used to get dogs to 'sit' or 'lie down' is 'tumbate!' said with authority. It is best to just ignore the dogs and to pretend that they are not there.

Opening and closing times:

The daily timetable in Spain differs markedly from that

of Britain and France. Cathedrals, churches, monasteries and museums open at 9 or 10 until 1.30 or 2pm and reopen around 4.30 or later. Summer opening times, where known, are given here. Winter, with its shorter opening times, is usually from October to March.

In most towns and villages there is an evening Mass at 8pm, occasionally 7.30 or 8.30, not at all in the smallest villages except on Sunday mornings. Many churches are kept locked and may not be opened to casual visitors, even those with good Spanish. Country churches are often cleaned on Saturday afternoons, which may give an opportunity to see the interior. Food can be bought up until 7.30 or 8pm but often not between 2 and 5pm.

In small villages you may have to ask where the shop is. This edition of the guide indicates the existence or not of shops in very small places. Lunch and dinner are served around 2pm and 9pm or later respectively. Fortunately, bars often have delicious 'tapas' or savoury snacks of many kinds, which help to fill gaps. If you are hungry at the wrong time for a meal, ask in a bar for 'unaracidn' of what you fancy and you will be given a full helping.

A Spanish sandwich is a 'bocadillo' and is also available at most times. Breakfasts in Spain are generally very modest, although some bars and hostals do a cooked breakfast after about 9.30. Note also that bars in some of the very small villages will not necessarily be open all the time, especially in spring and autumn.

Planning the Day:

It is important to plan each day, using this guide and your map.

The route in Spain is not easy and the Pyrenees are only the first of several mountain ranges you will encounter. An indication of the number of kilometres between places is given, and warnings of the more difficult stretches. Try to start at 6 or 6.30 (or earlier) in hot weather and have breakfast en route a bit later. It is also a good idea to stock up the night before with fruit or yogurts and plenty of water. If you can, reach your destination by 2pm in time for lunch and a rest in the hot part of the afternoon. You will then have time to visit places of interest in the town which will re-open around 5pm. In autumn it gets light quite late so if you are leaving early make sure you can see the yellow arrows. Cyclists should ensure that they can be seen by motorists on the roads. There are one or two days when walkers will need to carry a fair amount of food and water with them as shops are non-existent in some areas.

Prices:

Prices in Spain are now comparable with the rest of western Europe and hotel rates have risen quite rapidly in recent years. In restaurants the set 'menu del dia' is very good value and ranges from 700 to 1200 pesetas, with wine not always included in the cheaper menus. A full meal with wine, a Iacarte, tends to cost from 1700 pesetas upwards. Some 2000 prices are given as a guide to what you might have to pay in 2001. Breakfasts are not normally included in hotel room rates.

Returning from Santiago -

There are various ways of returning to the UK from Santiago, short of walking or cycling back, depending on the time and funds at your disposal.

By Air

Fly direct from Santiago. The Iberia Office in Santiago is atc/ General Pardinas 36, or their travel agents in Santiago: Viajes Piña, c/Republica de El Salvador 6, will book not only flights and all forms of travel.

By Coach

Eurolines and the Spanish company Alsa run coach services from Santiago to London and Paris for around 14,000 ptas. and also to Hendaye on the French/Spanish border. Alsa may take bikes for half the price of an adult ticket; if so you and your bike travel together.

The Eurolines coach to London is good and faster than going by train and ferry. If you decide to return by coach it is best to go in person to the Estacidn de Autobuses at San Cayetano, or you could try a travel agent first. A Dutch company has a special coach service known as the Fietsbus, which takes about 40 passengers and their bikes. The seats magically convert into two-tier, full-length beds at night and passengers are supplied with a blanket, pillow and slippers. The bikes are towed behind the bus in a large, purpose-built closed trailer. For further details and booking telephone the agents, Fietsvakantiewinkel, in Holland on (01031)-3480.21844 (if phoning from the UK).

By Train to France :

To find full timetables of both the regional and express trains and details of fares look up www.renfe.es. And for buses try www.alsa.es direct RENFE train runs between Santiago and Irun. Eleven and a half hours. To Bilbao ten and a half hours. To get to Santander change at Palcencia or Burgos. FEVE trains run along the north coast of Spain to Bikbao and Santander. A slow journey with beautiful scenery. Bicycles may be carried if space is available. You are advised to get a copy of the current rail timetable from the Tourist Office in Santiago or phone FEVE in Ferrol , tel: 981370433.

Suggestions on what walkers should carry

The cardinal rule here, is to travel as light as possible, many items you may feel are essential can be bought along the way, most villages have shops selling useful items.

Rucksack: Not more than 45 liters

Footwear: A pair of comfortable walking boots and an additional a pair of sandals.

Sleeping bag light with sleeping mat.

Sun Hat

Sun cream

Heavy Pullover for mountain areas

Swiss army knife

Water bottle large, a plate, knife and a spoon

One change of clothes, washing facilities are available in most places, so wear one wash one.

Guide Book & Map

Dictionary

A tent is not needed

Cooking equipment is not needed

Saint-Jean-Pied-de Port

Saint-Jean-Pied-de Port ("Saint John at the foot of the pass")
(163m)

This small, bustling and colourful town on the river Nive, is the capital of the Basque Province of Basse Navarre. It is also a major point of departure for pilgrims.

Madame Debril of the Societe des Amis de Saint-Jacques at 44 rue de Ia Citadelle, is a mine of valuable information and advice about the route. You are kindly advised to avoid calling on her too early in the morning, or after 7pm. She generally has an exhausting day generously imparting advice and guidance and is understandably strict about her hours of rest. If you have walked parts of the French route she will give you a stamp for her pilgrim record.

  Saint-Jean Pied-de-Port was central to the region of Cisa or the Merindad (administration) of Ultra Puerto. From the ninth century, it was the sixth Merindad of the kingdom of Navarre, connected with it by a common legal infrastructure. It was poetically described as the Garden of Navarre because of its refreshing and invigorating climate and its enchanting and idyllic vista of pastures and forests.

Under the Treaty of the Pyrenees it became a part of France in 1659. The town was much prized and lusted after by the Navarese kings. In the period of the Great Schism (1376-1417) it was declared an Episcopal see under the Pope of Avignon. There are a number of attractions. Citadelle, for instance, has a commanding view of the town. Its ramparts (accessible from the top end of the Rule de la Citadelle or by staircase, *escalier de la poterne*) can be reached from the footpath along the river by the side of the church. The climb on a clear day provides you with a stunning view. Also deserving of your interest are: Prison des Eveques, Musee de la Pelote, fourteenth century Eglise Notre-Dame du-bout-du-pont, Pont Romain and the different portes. The Basque-style houses some ornate wooden overhangs at roof level. Balconies are striking.

The very cooperative Tourist Office is happy to supply you with a pamphlet with marked walks in the area.

Accommodation:

For accommodation enquire of The Itzalpea, Ramuntcho and the Hotel des Remparts (opposite the public garden). Pilgrims may find the St Jean at Uhart-Cize on the western outskirts useful. The Hotel Camou, opposite the church, is friendly and hospitable. It is also noted for its wholesome food and safe storage for bicycles.

The realistic and un-bureaucratic Syndicate d'lnitiative (tourist office) is ready with information on chambres d'hote' (French bed and breakfast).

Keep an open mind and shop around carefully for clean, comfortable and economic accommodation and food. May we draw your discerning attention to: Refuge (6) at 55 rue de Ia Citadelle. It is managed and maintained by the Amis de la Vieille Navarre. The aforementioned Madame Debril is your contact. The gate d'etape at the house of Joseph Etchegoin (tel. 05 59.37.12.08) is the long-distance meeting point of the French GR65 and GR10. Campsite: Europ'Camping Cycle Repairs Ave du Jai Alai.

Directions:

The pilgrim has a choice of two routes:

<u>The Path over the mountains Route Napoleon</u>

(A) On taking your leave of Jean, follow the D428. At the village of Hauntto 5 Km from St Jean the road curves. Follow the arrowed path to the left and walk 25 km to Roncesvalles. The Route Napoleon (the Route du Marechal harrespe) is a much more demanding climb over the mountains. Do not take unnecessary risks. Prudence dictates that these potentially hazardous climbs be made in reasonably good weather. There is no substitute for mountain bikes. It has to be stressed that the cyclist should be fit because the course is exacting. The route is clearly sign posted and has yellow arrows to guide you. The unfit walker may take 12 hours to reach Roncevalles via this route.

<u>The route along the Road</u>

(B) This is the route via the main road for the elderly, unfit, or walkers with breathing problems. It is more hospitable in poor weather than the mountain path above. The road route via Arneguy, Valcarlos and the pass is also quite challenging.

Take the D933. After leaving St Jean-Pied-de-Port, get on the D933 with clear signs to Pamplona, Roncesvalles, and Spain. Cyclists may hear some frightening anecdotes about this leg of the journey, hard, arduous and steep. Don't be distracted or lose your concentration by the tales, some real, some apocryphal, about the less pleasant experiences of some pilgrims.

The first stretch of the route is problem-free. If the temperature is high, you can take a breather under shady spots, quite plentiful. These resting points have a generous water supply. After covering 8km of this route you enter the village of Arneguy. You can drink a beer or a glass of wine in the cosy bar. You can also pick up essentials in Arneguy's well-stocked and friendly shops. When you finally take your leave, you come to an abandoned customs post. You are now on Spanish soil. Bear in mind local sensitivities and salute the locals with *Hola!* not *Bonjour!* .

The road ascends steeply but is never intimidating. A reasonably fit person will take it in his or her stride. The road is neat and well surfaced with little traffic, save for the occasional timber truck. After 3 km you are in Valcarlos.

The bars of St Jean are not open in the early hours. Stock up on provisions the day before. Start early, preferably before midday, and make sure you have some bottles of water. During March and April watch out for melting snow. Tread or ride with care. On the Route Napoleon, Ronesvalles is about 27km from St Jean.

10km to Valcarlos
(365m) (Road route only)
Valcarlos is on the Spanish side of the border. There are shops, a tourist office and bank. Because of the bank's unusual opening hours, you may not be able to change money.

Most churches in this part of the old world, are associated with mythical or historic events. The most prominent local church, which you should try and visit, has an interesting history. It houses a polychrome sculpture of St James, said to be one of the conquerors of the Moors ("Santiago Matamoros"). Legend, especially in the Song of Roland, claims that Roland, probably a warrior, sounded his horn, "Oliphant", disturbing and alerting Charlemagne and his army who were resting nearby. The king, sensing trouble, instructed his troops to return to the battlefield immediately. They were late. Roland and his companions had been slain by Basque warriors in a surprise strike from the heights of Ibaneta.

In another more romantic legend, the "Bosque de las Lanzas Floridas " (Forest of the Flowering Spears), 53,000 intrepid maidens volunteered for Charlemagne's army. They were replacements for the warriors slaughtered in the bloody Basque onslaught.

Accommodation:

Hotel Maitena has a wonderful view from the dining room and offers meals from 10 Euros. Rooms for about 33 Euros. Hostal Casa Marcelino offers food. Casa Rural has double rooms for 33 Euros.

Directions:

The road gets steeper, but it's not a strenuous climb. When you leave Arneguy, and advance towards Ibaneta, you will notice yellow arrows and red "balises" of French way marking. This is a diversion designed with good intentions, primarily to shorten the distance. These "markers" can sometimes be confusing, especially in the thickets of a forest. Don't panic, be fully focused. Take the hilly road and descend to Puerto d'Ibaneta.

The climb starts in earnest for cyclists at Valcarlos. There are no villages for 17km. At Casa Guardiano you are 3km away from the summit. The road gets steeper. Quite a taxing climb and you will need to pause briefly and refresh your over-worked lungs. Take in more oxygen before you advance to the chapel on the "summit" of the Ibaneta Pass. Take advantage of the "summit's" two kind attributes; first a charming, serene view, and, second, the opportunity to tarry a while to wipe off the perspiration and inhale good, clean country air. The chapel is not always open, but you can see a collection of crosses and the monument to Roland.

14km to **Ibaneta**
(1057m)
Remember Roland's warning horn. It was from this village that he sent out his SOS. Sadly, when Charlemagne reached the place, the Basque armies had wiped out Roland and his men.
In poor weather conditions, the Charlemagne's chapel bells will ring to alert pilgrims. The old chapel, ruined beyond repair, gave way in 1965 to a new chapel. Signs in French, Spanish, Basque and Latin welcome pilgrims to prayer at the shrine of Our Lady of Ronceval. There is a modern monument to Roland.

Directions:
There is a delightful wooded walk, down the hill for the 2km to Roncesvalles. You are with Nature in its entire splendor and it's a brief but exhilarating experience. The path is waymarked: there are some small buildings on your right. Turn left and you arrive at a chapel. Just before you reach the abbey, the path merges with a track coming from the left. The monastery is a minute or so away. Go through a courtyard and you are face to face with the church.

3km to **Roncesvalles**
(952m, 42)
The Augustinian monastery is in the "valley of thorns" in the foothills of the Pyrenees.
From the eleventh century, the plain of Erro (Derivatives are Erro-zabal, Ronzabal, Roncesvalles) has been mute witness to Roland's fall at the hands of the Basques. A collection of medieval lyrics, *"chansons de geste"* recalls one of the most tragic episodes in European history.
  Sancho de Larossa, the Bishop of Pamplona, built a hospital here in the X11th Century. He was generously supported by Alfonso I "el Batallador" and some nobles. The hospital received *"pilgrims and others who might wish to lodge at the peak called Roncesvalles near the chapel of Charlemagne"* (the original chapel at Ibaneta). The papacy assumed responsibility for the maintenance and running of the hospital.
A twelfth century poem records that the hospital was "open to all, sick and well, not only Catholics but also pagans, Jews, heretics

and vagabonds.... women and men took it upon themselves to minister, doing so with great charity".

In 1132, the hospital was transferred to a site near the collegiate church where it still stands today, an inspiring reminder of medieval man's humanity to man.

Since it was founded by a chapter of Augustinians, it has been run by canons regular dependent on a sister house in Pamplona.

In 1984, the chapter passed, with papal authority, to the direct control of the archbishop of the city. The Prior continued using the medieval title of *Grand Abbot of Cologne*. A canon was given the title of *hospitalero,* with special responsibility for pilgrims. In the fifteenth century, the hospital was temporarily closed and some prime land in Castile and Aragon was sold. The estates also suffered two devastating fires (1445 and 1468). This setback only briefly interrupted the good works of the hospital. In the early seventeenth century it was revitalised. It is claimed that it provided 25,000 meals a year for pilgrims, rich and poor.

A very old building, some say the oldest in Roncesvalles, is the *Capilla de Sancti Spiritus or Silo de Carlomagno* (XII century). It is built over the graves of pilgrims who breathed their last in the area.

The thirteenth century *Capilla de Santiago* is much admired for its Romansque-Gothic architectural style. Visitors are struck by its unusual doorway. The reassuring and lively bell, whose joyous peals acted like a magnet for pilgrims from Ibaneta, hangs in the belfry.

The collegiate church, the creation of Sancho el Fuerte (1194-1215), was consecrated in 1219. It drew its inspiration from the churches of the Isle de France. With a French Gothic design, it is markedly distinctive, quite unlike contemporary Spanish architecture. The fires that were a constant hazard in the medieval era also reduced much of the collegiate church to ashes. It was lovingly and painstakingly restored in 1940.

Still surviving is the *Pantheon Real* or *Sala Capitular* (chapter house), (XIV). Also known as *La Preciosa* ("the beautiful"), it has a brilliantly sculptured thirteenth century mausoleum, the resting place of Sancho "el Fuerte" and his wife, Clemencia de Toulous. In 1600 the cloister was demolished by a severe fall of snow. The reconstruction was not of a high standard. This caricature offended many artistic and religious sensibilities.

There are no food shops in the area so take adequate precautions.

Accommodation: *Casa Sabina,* on the left at the entrance to the village, was highly thought of. It was comfortable, clean and relatively inexpensive. Sadly, it was closed in the summer of 2005. Is it now open?.

The new *La Posada,* is more expensive. Before 9.00pm during Mass, it offers a special pub meal for pilgrims. Some disgruntled customers complain that the meal is not "filling". The *La Posada.* (t:948-76 0225) has no bike shed.

We would unhesitatingly recommend the clean, comfortable and congenial *Real Colegiata* youth hostel in the old hospital. Dinner, bread and breakfast for one person around 5 Euros.

Refuge (36) at the monastery; bunks in two rooms, hot showers, kitchen (no pans).

Directions:
You will enjoy this comfortable and cool stretch. From Roncesvalles to the periphery of Pamplona large areas of shade protect you. In July/August the heat is intense but the considerate shade will keep you in a good and relaxed mood.

Depart from the monastery by the main entrance (KM47 on the N135), and turn first right into a footpath parallel to the road close to an information board. An interesting anecdote, perhaps an instructive one - in the 14th century, pilgrims usually crossed left on leaving the village. Modern pilgrims should continue along a path shaded by trees. This is roughly parallel with your starting point. This road descends gently. Stick to it.

About 2km later, you pass through a 2nd gate. Turn left to a track approaching from the right and rejoin the road at K47 close to the unmistakable HQ of the Guardia Civil. Turn right [RJ: turn left here]? and continue for 500 m to Burguete.

Cyclists should take the C135 road from Roncesvalles towards Pamplona. This is a good, generally well-surfaced road, which gently descends for 2km to the Basque village of Burguete.

3km to **Burguete**

(892m)

Very attractive, eighteenth,early nineteenth-century houses dominate both sides of the main street of this lovely Basque village.

Pharmacy and bank (closed in the afternoon for the civilised and celebrated siesta)

Accommodation: Hotel/restaurant Burguete (intelligent provision for bikes). A number of hostels.(t: 948-76 00 05). For those with a more generous budget, there are the Hotel Loizu Hs (t: 948-76 00 08) and Hotel Juandeaburre (t: 948-76 00 78) Hotel Loizu has single rooms for 28 Euros but without baths.

Campsite: Urobi at Espinal, (see below); class II site, open 1 April to 30 September.

Directions:

Go down the main street past the modern church of San Nicolas de Bari and the public garden. Do a right turn after 100m on the side of the bank building. Follow the track and cross. Go straight to the footbridge over the stream in the direction of UMUR (shades). Veer left to other UMUR (shades). This brings you to the road below the modern church of San Bartholomew and the tower of the *Bibliotheca Publica* on the other side of the road signposted to Espinal.

Cyclists have an easy time, going downhill. After 2.5km the road swings sharp right, a km before the ancient Basque village of Espinal.

3km to **Espinal**
(871m)

Basque village which proudly traces its origin to 1269. The homes, possibly as a deterrent to criminals or for macho militaristic reasons, proudly display some weapons above their doors.

Many pilgrims from European countries, plagued by high levels of crime, may probably sympathize with these deterrents, and express admiration for the creative spirit. If you have time, visit the modern church of St Bartholomew.

You have a small but interesting choice of bars, restaurants, panaderia shops.

Accommodation:
Campsite Urrobi. Open from April to September.

Directions:
Turn right on the main road in the village. Pass the fountain and turn left at house No.19 (Aunta Mendi) and take the small stretch of Macadamized road uphill. 200m later keep straight on left for UMUR. Proceed for about 100m, the road forks right to footpath, which takes you into the woods. It's uphill all the way to the top. The TV mast at Monte Orzanzurieta and Col Lepoeder rears its head over the foothills. Fork right at the top, turn left through gate and continue right along gravel lane. Keep straight on this lane with a fence on the side of the field. Leave the gate at end shaded by trees. Look left and right, concentrate, and when you are satisfied that it is safe to do so, cross the road at Alto de Mezquiriz.

Cyclists face a 12km ascent with some tricky hairpin bends leading to Alto de Erro.

2 km **Alto de Mezquiriz**
(922m)

A new sign invites the pilgrim in three languages, French,

Spanish and Basque to prayer at Notre-Dame de Roncevaux.
Directions:
After crossing the road do *not* go straight through the gate and up the track, though this might seem to be the thing to do. Go left down a small footpath before you reach the fence. Enter the gateway for the woods. The path veers right at a fork into a semi-shaded, undulating woodland. You thus avoid many of the hairpins on the road below. The left footpath takes you down through a gate to a lane advancing from the right. Take it and 60m later you reach a road at a bend. Take the old, shaded tunnel-like path, which metamorphoses into a lane. Turn left at fork with another lane coming from T and continue downhill to road at bridge over stream. [Right]: Turn left and then take left of two forks.

Turn right and continue on road for 100m then fork right down footpath, which becomes a lane. Continue across crash barrier at next bend. The road starts to climb again. Emerge on old main road in village of Viscarret.

5km to **Viscarret**
(780m)
Small village with shop and bar mark the end of the first stage of the Way of St James, described in the Codex Calixtinus.
Accommodation:
Casa Rural has double rooms for 32 Euros. Bar Juan serves meals, sandwiches and coffee. Pilgrim stamp from church.
Directions:
Turn right, cross main road (church above on left) and continue to end of village. Turn right, and then left down track, which takes you to the road about 200m later. Pass small cemetery on left, go down footpath to left of road. Rejoin the road, continue on it for 200m. Fork right down footpath, which becomes a green lane and go straight into the village of Linzoain.

1.5 km Linzoain
A most welcoming village for a rest. At the church on the hill,

you can relax in a shady place and have a cat's nap. On waking you take in some interesting views.

From here to the Alto de Erro the route climbs along a wooded ridge.

Directions:
Follow the road through village past Fronton, veer left at fountain, turn right uphill under footbridge over the road and keep straight on. 400m later cross minor gravel road and keep straight on left. You come to a slightly staggered crossing up stony lane, which becomes a footpath. It's uphill all the time.

Veer left onto wider track emerging from back right and fork right onto footpath. The red and white balises are more numerous than the yellow arrows. Emerge at fork of track and gravel road, and fork left up track with Camino "milestone" marker at start. Shortly afterwards cross a gravel road and carry on down shady lane.

This is where Roland eventually decided, alas too late, to blow his horn in a desperate attempt to attract the support of Charlemagne and his army.

At junction with (walkers') signpost (2Linzoain 5.7km, Erro 2.850, 0.30h, NA40) turn right and take left hand of two forks downhill. Follow line of HT pylons. 300 m further on you reach the road (C135) at Alto de Erro.

4km **Alto de Erro**
(801m)
Directions:
Cross the road. The stone construction opposite covers a former well, which provided much needed water for pilgrims of old. Keep straight on through more woods, ignoring turnings to left and right. After 1 km pass to the left of an old building; this is the *Venta del Caminante or Venta del Puerto,* a former pilgrim inn.

Continue downhill, keeping a close watch for the way marks. You get a view of Zubiri with its large magnesia factory. Follow the track, which gradually loses height, descending to the old medieval bridge over the Agra in Zubiri.

Cyclists should ignore the C127 to the left. Continue on the C135 on a sharp winding descent for 10 km until it reaches Zubiri.

4km to **Zubiri**
(526m)
In the Basque language, Zubiri means *village with the bridge*. The bridge itself was known as *el Puente de la rabia*. Legend has it that any infected animal that crossed the bridge three times was cured of rabies. The large building immediately to the right before the bridge was a former hospital, probably a leprosarium.

Accommodation:
Casa Ceribi, double room 35 Euros; you may find some rooms at the Restaurant Gau-Txori at eastern end of village. Good food, no set menu and prices far from reasonable. Landlady Senora Romona Guelbenzo de Santestebin may be able to provide accommodation: take the first real left turn after bridge and knock on second door on left. Casa Valentina (t: 948-30 40 09) is a restaurant which may help you secure accommodation. Bar Gau Txori (t: 948-30 40 76) on south side of village, off the main street, serves good 'bocadillos'. Pass the medieval bridge for the

local shop located under sign on right. The new Refuge is in a renovated school. Bunks, kitchen and hot showers, 10 Euros a night. Key from parish priest or at 'panaderia' (baker).

Directions:
To get to the village cross the bridge (fountain on the other side next to a church). Or turn left along path just before the bridge (way marked). Go up hill and down the side of a large house. Cross stream by footbridge and keep straight on. Veer to right. At the "T" junction on gravel road near a factory, turn right and go left downhill on tarmac road and pass left of factory. Road climbs and when you are level with the last factory-building, fork right onto a track parallel to both road and electricity cables (between the two). You are now above and parallel with the river Agra in the valley below you to the right.
Towards end of factory at junction, another track comes from back right. Go down some steep steps following line or electricity cables. Cross road at bottom and keep straight ahead. Cross the stream and keep straight down the foot path (parallel to and between two sets of electric cables). This leads uphill between banks to merge at side of house in the hamlet of Ilarratz. Turn left at fountain and then right down minor tarred road. At bend in road (signposted "Eskirotz 500m") keep straight on uphill left to hamlet. Fork left at end along walled lane with fields below to your right. Keep straight on. Pass battery hen farm, as track becomes UMUR and keep straight on to minor road. Cross it, go up a short flight of steps and keep straight onto footpath through field, which continues alongside another footpath between banks. Track climbs up and down, joined by another from back shortly before you reach a minor road at entry to village of Larrasoana.
Cyclists should continue down the valley along the river to their left.

5km to **Larrasoana**
The village church began as a monastery. It was later donated to Leyre. The charitable hospitals served pilgrims. There is a statue of St James in the church. No shop or restaurant. The bar

next to the refuge will prepare meals if you order in advance. The next welcoming bar (with tapas) is in Urdaniz, 2km north on the C135.

Accommodation:
Refuge: Modern new refuge for 30 persons, a thoughtful initiative by the genial and hospitable mayor (*alcalde*) Don Santiago Zubiri Elizalde. He is well liked by pilgrims, a most helpful person. Situated in the town hall, the refuge has a kitchen and hot and cold showers. Canned and fresh foods available. After normal hours, the key can be got from the mayor in the house opposite. Camping space available.

Directions:
To enter village turn right, cross bridge and then turn left at church. Turn left onto road and proceed to the hamlet of Aquerreta. There is a fountain 1km away. Keep straight on down green lane to house with old weapons on its door. This house was probably built in 1747. Go downhill, cross minor tarred road at slightly staggered junction and keep straight on lane. The track takes you in and out of woods, parallel all the time with the main road below you to the right. Path descends steeply down steps. Continue close to and parallel with river, passing weir on right. Shortly after, you get to a modern bridge over the Agra at Zuriain.

4.5 km **Zuriain**
Directions:
Cross bridge and veer left onto main road (N135). Continue along main road for 300m and turn left down minor road signposted to "Illlurdoz3". Cross bridge over the Arga, back on to the left hand bank again. Immediately after, turn at bend on road. Continue on path to village of Irotz (2km). Veer right round side of large white house, pass front of church to your right and Kso on concrete road. Cross medieval bridge back over the river again to the village of Uroz. Turn left onto footpath parallel to road and between road and river. Continue to village of Zabaldica.

3km **Zabaldica**

The local church houses a statue of St James. This is usually locked. If you want to see this well sculpted statue you can obtain the key from a nearby house. To get to the church turn right in middle of tarred road and cross main road after 20m.
Directions:
Continue for 200m on footpath then rejoin road (N135). Cross over and fork right uphill on footpath just before road KM9 and the old road bridge over the Agra. Track continues parallel to river. (*From here you can see the village of Huarte in the distance to your* left *and the Romanesque Ermita de la Virgen de la Nieve* **over on the hill on the opposite side of the river**). Follow the way marks into fields for 1 km until you get to the main road. It's a busy road, exercise great care when crossing. The more wary pilgrim has the alternative of a tunnel under the road (a concrete tube). Turn right into the service road. This veers left and after a few hundred yards you reach a bridge over the river Ulzama (a tributary of the Arga) at Trinidad de Arre.

3.5km **Trinidad de Arre**
Accommodation:
Refuge (22) at Basilica de Arre. Hot showers and kitchen. 6 Euros. Meals can be had from Circulo Catolico and Hostal Obelix 7 Euros Menu.
Directions:
On your right, immediately after the bridge is the Basilica de la Sanctissima Trinidada, the site of a small pilgrim hospital in the old days. Turn left after crossing the bridge (fountain on right) and you are in Villava.

0.6 km **Villava**
Villava is a suburb of Pamplona.
Directions:
Go along main street for 1 km past public garden (left) and bear (right). Cross the roads at traffic lights. Continue straight along a tree-lined paseo and you are in the suburb of Burlada.

1km **Burlada**
There are a few shops and some may cater to your

requirements.
Directions:
You come to a set of traffic lights. There is a Michelin tyre dealer on your right, and the Villa Josepha with a garden full of old, attractive trees. A word of warning - do *not* continue straight ahead towards the road bridge. Cross the road and turn right along the Calle Larraizar. There's a school on the right, just before you reach the main road. Cross the road, keep straight on the other side along a small tree-lined road , the Camino or Carretera Burlada for 2km. Ignore first left hand fork in road.
(As you proceed you get a rewarding view of Pamplona cathedral. On the left *there are two houses with facades adorned with scallop shells)*
As you get close to the river (fountain on right by school), a minor road runs across. Turn right and take a quick left over the Puente de los Peregrinos. This is the old pilgrim bridge over the river Arga and has acquired a good-humored notoriety for a recently decapitated statue of St. James perched on a small column at the far end.
Follow way marks and cross the public garden towards the town walls. Cross at diagonally right traffic lights. Don't deviate - walk between the inner and outer sets of ramparts. At the gateway take the rising Calle del Carmen into the old quarter of Pamplona.

20km to **Pamplona**
Pamplona (population 200.000) is the first big city on the route. Quite modern with a fairly advanced tourist infrastructure. There are buses to Burguete, Puenta la Reina, Estella, Logrono. A map shop opposite the cathedral is helpful.
Tourist Offices: an enlightened office on right-hand side of main road as one nears the city. Main TO is on the Calle Ahumada, east of the central Plaza del Castillo.
Pamplona belongs to the Roman era and is said to be founded by Pompey. The first documented references to this fascinating town have been attributed to Strabo, the classical geographer and historian. Charlemagne destroyed the city in 778. The

Basques avenged this vandalism with their stunning defeat of an important part of his army at Roncesvalles.

The eleventh century witnessed the dramatic development of Pamplona as it expanded into attractive suburbia for the many foreigners, particularly the French, to settle there. The Navarese, who occupied part of the city, gave it the eponymous label, Navarreria.

San Fermin was the city's first Bishop and Patron. His feast is regularly celebrated on 7 July. This is followed by the famous or the infamous (depending on your attitudes to animals and humans!) bull- running week chronicled by the macho Ernest Hemingway, who had little regard for the "sentimental" anti-blood sports and feminist lobby. Times have greatly changed since then, and Hemingway is no longer held in awe, especially by the new more articulate and efficiently organised generation of ecology and animal rights activists.

The medieval period was plagued by conflict and confrontations between the native population and the more privileged burghers from elsewhere. The old town was ruined during The Civil War in 1276. The famous *privilegio de la Union,* granted by Carlos

III on 8 September 1423, put an end to the rivalries. Later, the city was refortified.

We recommend a visit to the gothic cathedral. This is built on the supposed site of the Roman capital. The "new" cathedral replaces a Romanesque one said to be designed by Master Esteban. It was commissioned by the imperious Sancho "el Mayor" (1100-1127). Dating from the fourteenth and fifteenth centuries, the cathedral is built on a Latin cross design. It has three aisles. In the eighteenth century a neoclassical façade, designed by Ventura Rodriguez, heightened its splendour. The north tower is home to the second largest bell in Spain. Weighing twelve tons, it was cast by Pedro de Villanueva in 1584.

Above the high altar is the eye-catching image of Virgen del Sagrario or Santa Maria la Real. The kings of Navarre swore their oaths in front of this image. The Child was added to this venerated figure, but both are overshadowed by a neo-gothic baldachin.

A fifteenth century alabaster mausoleum of Carlos III "el Noble" and his wife Leonora of Trastamara is prominently positioned in the main nave. Experts describe it as a jewel of Gothic funerary art.

The grille across the entrance to the chancel is also very

attractive, flamboyant and gothic. The highly talented Guillermo Ervenat created it in 1517.

The Gothic cloister on the square plan is a most imaginative architectural work.

Those with a strong interest in paintings and sculpture should take in The Diocesan Museum with its very impressive collection from the fourteenth to the sixteenth centuries. There is some delightfully unusual metalwork.

The Hospital of San Miguel adjoins the cathedral. Constructed in the eleventh century, it is celebrated for the humane thirteenth century activities of Bishop Miguel Sanchez de Uncastillo. He provided 50 beds for the use of pilgrims, every one of whom was supplied with bread, wine, and a plate of vegetables and meat. The pilgrim's kitchen, with its central chimney, still exists. Hospitals were located at number 13 calle Dormitaleria and number 3 Compania. At a time when robbers and brigands ruthlessly preyed on defenceless pilgrims, the pilgrims resting in San Miguel were safe under the special protection of what were regarded as the city's law enforcement officers.

The 16th century *Hospital de Nuestra Senora de la Misericordia,* now the Museum of Navarre, still retains its charming platersque doorway. Here are Navarre exhibits, artistic and archaeological, of different periods. The eleventh century ivory casket carved in Cordoba and transported to Navarre will delight you. There's even a Goya portrait of the Marquis de San Adrian (1804).

The *Church of San Cernin* or *San Saturnino* of Toulouse is a monument to the city's evangelist and patron. Outside, a marker indicates the position of the well used by the saint to baptise the city's first Christians. This Romanesque church was rebuilt in the thirteenth century. The north tower with battlements, which survived into the eighteenth century, had martial overtones. The eighteenth century baroque chapel of the Virgen del Camino is a reminder of an age when artists and builders put the spiritual above the material. A statue of St James in his pilgrim role (*Santiago Peregrino*) is in the facade.

The renaissance retable in the church of Santo Domingo (XVI

century) is dominated by a representation of Santiago Apostil. Also depicted is the legend of the donkey stolen from a family of pilgrims. Thanks to the saint's intervention, the family got their donkey back. A number of tombs are of historical importance.

The Camera de Comptos was the ancient Chancellor's court. It is now the headquarters of the Principle de Viana Institute. This small building is an endearing example of 13th-X1Vth Pamplona's civil Gothic style. In 1868 it was declared a national monument. Part of it abuts on to the city wall, built as a protection against invaders.

If you are looking for paintings of high artistic and material value, you will find many in the mid-nineteenth century, neoclassical style Palace of Navarre. The royal archives contain first-rate documentary sources for the Spanish medieval period. Fascinating, too, are the *Liber Regalis* or ceremonial book of the English court (XVIth century) and the enamel chalice, which Carlos III presented to the Virgin of Ujue.

The University of Navarre in Pamplona is regarded as one of Spain's leading universities.

Accommodation:

Refuge: (24) Refugio Iglesia San Cernin. Open from May to October. (70) Albergue Amaiur with hot showers and no kitchen. Open in July and August.1200 - 2130.

Ezcaba campsite tel:948330315 is beyond Oricain out of town. 8.5 km. on the N121 to Irun. Open from June to September. Pension Lambertini, Calle de Mercadores 17, tel: 948 21 03 03, is in the city on the pilgrim route and charges 4000 for a double room. Pension Arrieta, c/Arrieta 27, has double rooms for 25 Euros. bikes accommodated. Hotel La Perla has single rooms for 18 Euros. tel: 948 22 77 06. Ernest Hemingway stayed in this hotel in room 217. Hotel Eslava, Plaza Virgen de la O,7, tel: 948 22 34 28 has double rooms for 35 Euros.

Hotel Fonda, accommodation something of a problem. Exasperatingly expensive between 1 and 15 July (festival of San Firmin and the 'running of the bulls'). The calle San Nicolas has a number of bars. Most are rowdy, and some have their own share of lager louts, mostly foreigners, heartily despised by the locals. The bars are not as cheap as they once were. The ghost of the thirsty Hemingway will be outraged. Bar Gallego. 10 Euros. El Labrador, pilgrim menu for 10 Euros. Restaurante Sarasate is Vegetarian.

Try no.25, the Bearan, with a 2nd floor patio for bicycles. Also give the Calle San Esteban a try. If you are still "homeless" and insecure, enquire at the Hostel Ibarra, Calle Estafeta 85, near the bullring. In 1993 the Hotel Lorca, on the main square, won some accolades; it was praised for its quiet and comfort. The Restaurante El Redin, Calle del Mercado, near Museo de Navarra, serves good food. (850-peseta menu).

1) Trinidad de Arre convent on the river Ulzama, just before the Villava bridge as you enter Pamplona. Beds, hot showers and kitchen. Forty-five minute walk into the city.

2) Pamplona refuge, next to San Cernin is very good, with 20 bunk beds, 2 showers and kitchen. Limited space for bikes. 6 Euros.

Campsite:
Ezcaba at Oricain, 7km north of Pamplona on the N121 road to Irun; shop, bar and swimming pool, open 1 June to 25 September.

Cycle Repairs:
Bicicletas Alberto, Calle Monasteno de Urdax 23, tel. 948.17.26.09; Reparacion Bicicletas, Calle Monasteno lranzu 5, tel. (948) 27.62.77; Ciclos Olite, Calle Alfonso Beorlegui 50, tel. (948) 11.72.29.

Directions:
The route is way marked through Pamplona with blue and yellow plaques bearing the Council of Europe's *path of the stars* motif. Your guiding "star" is the "point" of the cluster. There are many such plaques along the camino. Most are for decorative purposes, and are of no help in plotting your way.

To reach the cathedral, turn off the Calle del Carmen at a small square with a statue.

Keep straight on along the Calle del Carmen, turn right into the Calle de Mercadores, continue to the Plaza Consistorial, turn right into the Calle san Saturnino and keep straight on to the

Calle Mayor. Go straight on, and pass left of a public garden. At the crossing of Avenida Pius XII and Avenida Jaconera, veer left to parkland surrounding the Cuidadela and follow the flagstone path (way marked). When it turns in front of the Cuidadela, swing right across the grass to the road.

Cross and continue down the Calle Fuente de Hierro. This leads downhill under the road bridge across the campus of the University of Navarre, and becomes the Camino de Santiago.

Continue along a minor road signposted "Cizor Menor". Cross the bridge, first over the river Sadar, and then the rive Elorz. Proceed. When the modern road forks to the left, fork right, keep straight on. Cross the busy railway track with care. Or, go up steps to the road (both options join up 100 m later) Continue and this path develops into a pavement along the main road to the left, which it joins. Go to the top of the hill descending to the village of Cizur Menor.

Cyclists are warned. It is difficult to get your directions right with a street map of Pamplona. Many one-way streets and intersecting medieval streets can add to your frustration. The Pamplona route is not easy to find. There are no signposts in the centre. It is only when you discover the correct exit, after a possibly exhausting search, will you find the N111 (Puenta La Reina) signpost to the outskirts. The citizens are helpful to strangers and you are advised to stop and ask for directions. Once you are on the N111 and cross the route, the rest is easy.

4km to **Cizur Menor** (from Pamplona)

Small village, bar, restaurant (but no shop), fountain in public garden (right)

The church of St John of Jerusalem belonged to the Order of the same name. It was built at the end of the twelfth century. The pentagonal cloister was added between 1250-1265, with the conventional buildings. From the beginning, it had an efficient, clean and caring pilgrim hospital. In 1508 it had a house " with six beds where poor pilgrims can sleep and be rested." Its fortunes seriously declined as a result of the misappropriation. The only survivor was the church, but it was neglected. It was even converted into a warehouse. It has been restored. The doorway is Romanesque, with the Greek monogram of Christ in the tympanum. The Romanesque parish church, also restored, is on the right.

Accommodation:
Splendid refuge run by the Roncals, a kind and hospitable family, well known in the village. Refuge (16) has wooden bunks with curtains and a clean and well-equipped kitchen. 6 Euros a night. Refuge (16) run by Knights of St John of Malta. Open from June to September. 7 Euros. Restaurant Asador el Tremendo, 10 Euros menu. Behind the farmacia is a bar which serves meals.
Cycle Repairs: Ciclos Cizur, Calle Mirador, tel. (948) 17.22.82.

Directions:
Go downhill, and 100 m later fork right down footpath, down left hand side of the *fronton* and turn left. Proceed straight to road, which becomes UMUR. (*The Monte del Perdon (1.037m) and a line of forty modern windmills along a ridge to its right are visible. They are the energy source of Pamplona's electric power grid*).
Join Macadamized road approaching from left and continue. 100 m later (road bends right); keep straight on (left) on UMUR. When this bends to right after 200m, turn left to clear footpath through fields under electric cables. This takes you to the church and village of Guendulain. About 200m later, cross minor tarred road. Go straight uphill.
Ignore left turn at junction lined by four large trees. Just before a group of eight trees UMUR bends left. Keep right on earth track at junction with UMUR (small lake/reservoir to left) go left up hill. At next crossing 60m later, proceed straight towards windmills on skyline. You get a good view of Pamplona. Continue uphill to Zariegui.

6km **Zariegui**
570m (813)
Continue straight through village (Romanesque church on right) on a UMUR (in the direction of the windmills all the time). 500 m after village, ignore left turn but take left fork at "Y" junction

20m later. Steep uphill road (a lonely tree on right hand side of path as you go upward is an ideal resting place under evening sun} Proceed straight.

You come to a splendid fountain (it does not always work). Then there's a spot named Gambellacos. Legend has it that a tired and thirsty pilgrim making his way up to the Alto del Perdon was confronted by the devil disguised as a walker. The devil offered to show him a hidden fountain on the strict condition that he renounces God, the Virgin Mary and St James. The pilgrim spurned the devil. St James, disguised as a pilgrim, came to his rescue and led him to a hidden fountain where he was able to quench his thirst with the help of his scallop shell.

5km **Alto del Perdon**
780m (818)

Exciting panoramic views as you head towards Puenta la Reina. Methodically laid out in front of you are the villages you will pass through - Uterga, Muruzabal and Obanos. At the crossing you will find the "Parque Eolico del Perdon" created in 1996. This is a most delightful picnic spot with cast-iron "cut-out" sculptures of pilgrims on foot and horseback and two donkeys and a dog! The inscription reads, *donde se cruza el Camino del viento con el de las estrellas* (where the path of the wind crosses that of the stars), a poetic reference to the Camino de Santiago and the Milky Way.

Directions:

Get to the other side of the road following the way marks, which lead to the valley bottom. You now join a track coming from behind on the right and keep straight on (left). Cross a small river with a long line of trees along its banks and walk uphill into village of Uterga.

3km to **Uterga**
(824)

Tiny village down side road. Cyclists go left. The community bar is open only in the evenings. (It does not serve food, drinks only.) Pilgrims can stay in community hall. Casa Baztan serves

food. The La Sociedad Bar serves drinks.
Directions:
Go straight through village and continue along quiet road to Muruzabal.

3km **Muruzabal**
(824)
Bar, fountain.
Directions:
After leaving the village take a right turn diagonally and then just before you come to a roadside cross walk along the side of fields. You will notice a road coming up on the left which you should join and walk straight on. At the top of the hill, take the right fork right which will lead you into Obanos.

2km to **Obanos**
414m (826)
At Ermita San Salvador, another road from Arles joins the route from Roncesvalles over the Somport pass. A short detour takes you to the twelfth-century church at Eunate, 3 km away on the Monreal Las Campanas road. It is an octagonal building surrounded by a series of arches. It was a burial place for pilgrims. While most

pilgrims completed the journey safely, some succumbed to illness and others were fatally injured in accidents.

Accommodation:
Bank, restaurant, panaderia. Restuarant Ibarberoa is behind the church. Hospederia Arnotegui; Casa Pepe restaurant, not easy to identify but worth the enquiry. It is noted for its tasty, homemade meals.

Directions:
Enter the village by the Camino Roncesvalles. Proceed straight to Calle San Juan; turn right into Calle Julian Gayarre, left down a tree-lined road with a school (left) to church (public garden on its right). Continue diagonally through archway and go straight, following road as it bends to right passing fountain opposite. At the Ermita San Salvador (left) the road becomes a rough track at the side of the farm (right). Keep straight on above vines (to left) until you come to the main road. Cross, turn left down footpath through allotments. A wall and fencing run parallel to road. Rejoin road by hotel. There is a modern statue of a pilgrim at the junction of the Caminos Frances and Aragones. Turn left along the N111 for 300m to Puente le Reina (Gares).
Cyclists can turn off the N111 immediately after the summit of the Puerto del Perdon and enter a quiet road through Uterga and Muruzabal.

2km to **Puente Ia Reina**
(346m,)
All facilities. Buses to Estella, Logrono and Pamplona.
Puente La Reina, or *Ponte de Arga,* got its name at the beginning of the eleventh century. Dona Major, wife of Sancho "el Major" (though she may also have been Dona Estefania, Dona Majore's niece) was the queen who gave her name to the town. She built the bridge over the river Arga for the use of pilgrims going to Compostela.
A French colony was firmly in place by 1090. Alfonso Garcia VI and I "el Batallador" played a central role in the town's development. Garcia VI handed it over to the Templars in 1142 and granted them some privileges. They continued to provide

free lodging for pilgrims.

When the Order of the Templars was destroyed, their possessions passed to the Order of St John of Jerusalem. Around 1469, Prior John Beaumont began building a new pilgrim hospital in the church of Crucifixion.
The town's principal monuments are to be found in a part of the callle de los Peregrinos, between the church of the Crucifixion and the famous bridge.
The church of Santa Maria de la Vega y del Crucicijo is Romanesque. The doorway was built in the thirteenth century. The gothic crucifix carried from Germany by a pilgrim is housed in the nave in the north side, a fifteenth century addition. The adjacent building and the top section of the tower were eighteenth century improvements.
The Romanesque image of the Virgen de la Vega is one of the oldest in Navarre.
The church of Santiago, the ancient parish church, retains only the twelfth century south door from the original structure. The important fifteenth century renovations gave it a high and spacious nave; the neoclassical tower was added in 1777. It contains a good polychrome wooden statue of Santiago Peregrino (XVI century).

The calle Major contains a notable group of monuments: at the near end it is flanked by two towers. On both sides all the way there are palaces, nobly proportioned houses with shields, projecting eaves and graceful balconies. The facades of the churches of the Trinity and Santiago also demand your attention. At the other end, a fortified gateway gives access to the Romanesque bridge. This is the pilgrim's bridge, one of the most interesting on the whole way to Santiago. The bridge gave its name to the town. It has six arches, and is a superb example of medieval construction, one of the few built during the period that survives in perfect condition.

Directions:
Turn left at Refugio, a two-storey building on the corner run by the Padres Reparadores, with an arcaded verandah outside, and

then turn right in front of the seminary, passing between it and the church of Santiago (right). Keep straight on down the Calle Mayor until you get to the old bridge over the Arga. Cross it and turn left on to road. Cross main road (near modern bridge) and fork left onto minor road, parallel to main road. When this veers right, back towards the main road at large wayside cross (picnic area, fountain). Fork left onto UMUR, which then becomes a cart track, running parallel to the river. Continue along it for 1.5 km and at a modern (water or electricity) tower across on the other side of the river to your left, you will see a path turning to your right onto a wide track. Take it, go uphill, forking left shortly afterwards to a ravine and then follow it (now a foot path) uphill again, turning right after a flight of steps onto a wide earth track leading steeply uphill. Pass site of former thirteenth-century Monasterio de Bargota (fountain, picnic area and orientation plan on main road above you to right) and continue on UMUR parallel to road until you enter village of Maneru.

4km to **Maneru**
(823)
Note medieval *cru cero* (wayside cross) at entrance, moved when

the road was widened.
Near the church there are two bars and two shops selling food.

Accommodation:
Hostal Puente, Paseo de los Fueros, is good value but can be noisy. Bikes may be kept in the utility room. The Meson Peregrino is comfortable but expensive, Fonda El Gares (on the bypass) is good and the Fonda Lorca does excellent meals.
Turismo in Plaza Mena. Tel:948 34 08 45 Open Tues-Fri 1000-1900 & Sat-Sun 1000-1400. Hostal Jakue has a dormitory for 20 in the basement, 16 Euros. Hot showers, supper from 1900 at 7 Euros. Hotel Rural Bidean Calle Mayor 20. Tel: 948 34 11 56 has rooms for 80 Euros. On the main road Meson del Peregrino tel: 948 34 00 75 has a pool. Rooms are for 70 Euros. Hotel Jakue Irunbidea has double rooms for 80 Euros. and 10 Euros for menu. Two good bars are Charlie Bar and Bar Yony. Bar la Torreta has 10 Euros. menu and is open at 0630 in summer. Puente H (T:948-34 01 46), Lorca F (T:948-34 01 27), Meson El Peregrino H (T:948-34 00 75)
Refuge: the refuge (33) of the Padres Reparadores is about 100 yards from the monastery on the way in to town. Bunk beds, no kitchen. Space to camp at the back. Ask at seminary for key.
Campsite: El Molino at Mendigorria, 6km south of Puente; class I site, open all year and good for the whole Roncesvalles to Logrono area; recommended, but may be expensive for walkers and cyclists.

Directions:
Fork left down road (marked *Yesos Pamplona*). This leads to gypsum factory. Continue downhill, fork right over bridge, cross triangular "square" and continue along the Calle de la Esperanza into the Plaza de los Fueros and the Casa Consistorial; houses with blazons. Turn left at end, then right and continue on Calle Forzosa/Camino de Santiago straight through fields. (a charming view of Ermita de Aniz on the hillside above to the right.) Pass cemetery (on your left). Keep straight on; track joins from back left shortly after. Stick to this road, which forks left. Turn left at "T" junction and right immediately after onto footpath, between hedges, walls and fields. This takes you to the hilltop village of

Cirauqui.

3km to **Cirauqui**
498m (835)
This well-restored ancient village also makes concessions to modernity. There is a shop, bar, and a fountain in the public garden. (You will find them 100m away on right side of main road). The Gothic church of San Roman may be worth a visit.
Some may have difficulties with the route through Cirauqui. Negotiating the yellow arrow indicators may be slightly irritating. However, try and keep a level head, go round the base of the village in a clockwise direction and continue along the straight line you took when you entered.

Directions:
When you reach the village continue between houses. Turn right, then left up steps and stick to this path with a staggered junction. Go up unnamed street under arch of tower to the top of a steep street. Turn left on the top into the Plaza and go under arch with stone seats. This is a pleasant, cool place for a rest. On the other side, turn left downhill and right down Calle de Mediodia, second left downhill. Veer right to join road coming

from back left. This becomes a track. Follow this tree lined track downhill onto old paved Roman road which leads you over the river on the old bridge. Continue till you reach the main road again, at roundabout/turning area.

Cross the road and turn left a few yards later onto earth road. This continues parallel to main road below to your left. Follow it as it undulates through fields, passing bridge on site of Gothic bridge and medieval route on line of Roman road.

On reaching the brow of the hill (view to main road), turn right down footpath by HT pylon. Veer left along edges of fields. Continue to junction with minor road to your right marked *Monasterio de Alloz* and *Embalse de Alloz* (a reservoir). Turn right on road, follow it under modern aqueduct, and pass houses on left. Turn left through two green gates onto a path, which goes over an old bridge.

The river Salado ("Salt River"), runs below this bridge. The waters of these rivers are dangerously unhealthy. Humans and animals were warned to steer clear of them by the safety conscious and perceptive Aimery Picaud. Death, he warned would come swift, to anyone who ignored this prohibition. Piccaud left a salutary reminder of the pitfalls. He says he saw two Navarese sitting on the riverbank sharpening their knives in anticipation of flaying pilgrim's horses which drank from the poisonous waters. Piccaud had learned the hard way, his own horse was a victim.

Take the path from the bridge and it will lead you under the modern road. On the other side, go right up old road and you are on your way to the village of Villatuerta.

7km to **Lorca**
(483m)(842)
Bar (a shy place almost afraid of advertising its presence-weekends only), fountain, rooms.

A pilgrim hospital served pilgrims and the local community in the thirteenth century. Impressed by its good works, Teobaldo 1, left the hospital a legacy in 1270. The church off Santa Maria with a Romanesque apse and Gothic nave was constructed in 1209. Some notable architectural elements were added in the sixteenth century.

A processional cloister was created beside the church in the flamboyant Gothic style of the fifteenth century. This is unlike that of the monastery of Monte Olivia in its configuration of space and decoration. The door of the church, beautifully designed and harmoniously proportioned, is plateresque. The renaissance-style tower, with a square base and an octagonal upper part, dates from the sixteenth century.

The choir stalls (1561) are most handsome. The Gothic painted panels of the altarpiece of the chapel of Eulate (XVI century) are very striking, excellently composed and coloured. This is particularly true of the two figures representing the Visitation. The main altarpiece and its wings are baroque and the polychrome wood figure of Santa Maria is fifteenth century gothic.

Directions:

Go through village past church (on your right) and down main street to road. Continue to top of hill. Turn left, then right along path boardered by cornfields and parallel to road. Follow track to village of Villatuerta.

4.5km to **Villatuerta**
(846.5)

Directions:

Cross old bridge and veer left uphill to church (ideal for a rest, pleasant views.) There is a fountain with safe drinking water behind church. Continue in front of church, veering right. At road fork, turn right and join main road 50m later (opposite the Ega Pan bread and cake factory). Turn left (2 bars 30m to right next to car wash), and 20m later cross over main road. Go up lane at right hand side of first house to left of bread factory. Veer left and go uphill under electric cables.

Follow this path uphill past farm building and fields. As it starts to descend, turn right along a footpath on an embankment above an olive plantation (partial view of Estella ahead). Keep straight, veering left all the time, round and above fields. On level with allotments, the footpath becomes a green line. Go straight downhill, surface becomes concrete, winding its way up and down alongside high wall/embankment (welcome seat to right at top of hill by junction). This descends to join minor road. Enter Estella on main road at bend in river Ega. (Right). Turn left up road marked to "Servicio Provincial de Incendios" (fire station)]

4.5km **Estella** (Lizarra)
426m (851/644)
Population 13,000. Modern facilities. Hotels, buses to Pamplona, Puenta La Reina, Logrono. Tourist Office: Calle San Nicolas 3.
Picturesque town with a charter going back to 1090. Sancho Ramirez established a French settlement near the church and Plaza of San Martin of Lizarra. This village, of little significance, bears traces of its Roman origins. The foundation and expansion of the city was the result of close co-operation with the Camino de Santiago.

At the end of the twelfth century, it occupied the area that presently comprises the historic centre. New neighbourhoods were created, churches built and hospitals established by several confraternities. For a long time, French and Jewish settlers lived in constant rivalry with the native townspeople. The appalling massacre of 1328 was the first of many cruel blows inflicted on the town. Floods and epidemics in the fifteenth century reduced it to a ghost town. In the nineteenth century, it was the court and residence of the Carlist kings, giving Estella a reputation, deserved or undeserved, as one of the most royalist and reactionary parts of Navarre.

Numerous monuments testify to the important role played by the city through the centuries.
San Pedro de la Rua has three gothic naves with an exceptional entrance showing Morisco and Cistercian influence. The central apse is late Romanesque. The demolition of the castle (carried out by Felipe II in 1572 so that it could not be used against him) crushed two sides of the twelfth century Romanesque cloister. The latter's beautiful capitals were decorated with botanical and animal subjects and those of the New Testament and hagiography. The entrance to the church is polluted and reminiscent of the one at San Roman at Cirauqui. One of the cloister's capitals, on a twisted column, is similar to one at Santo Domingo de Silos. The church contains the image of Nuestra Senora de Bele (XII century), formerly in the church of Santo Sepolcro.
San Miguel, founded in 1195, has a door with three archivolts and illustrative capitals with sculptured panels of the highest aesthetic quality. In the tympanum is a magnificent late Romanesque Christ Pantocrator with the Evangelists. Inside there is an interesting altarpiece (1406) with a statue of St Michael in the flamboyant gothic style. The whole church has a fortified air
.
The monastery of Santo Domingo was founded by Teobaldo II in 1259 and became a royal palace under Carlos II *el Malo*. The wall was built for king Luis Huntin in 1307 to separate the monastery from the adjacent ghetto.
The church was built from 1260 onwards on three levels to allow for the uneven ground. The Principe de Viana Institute restored it. In documents belonging to the cathedral of Pamplona, allusion is made to "the church of San Jayme of the Preaching

Brothers of Estela".This may perhaps be its original name on the Camino de Santiago.

Renovations to the church of San Juan Bautista have been so numerous that it is hard to imagine the early structure which was similar to that of Irache. The north side has a late Romanesque door (XII and XIII centuries) and the south side a gothic one (XIV century). The main façade is neoclassical (XVI century) and the towers are modern. Inside are a renaissance altarpiece and a beautiful statue of Nuestra Senora de las Torchas. These were restored in the 1950s in wood covered with silver. The church has a small museum of historical objects.

The convent of Santa Clara was founded in 1290 by Bernard Montaner, and finished in 1635. The church has the ground plan of a Latin cross with barrel vaulting. Some of the princes of Navarre were educated here.

The convent of the Concepcionistas Recoletas has a seventeenth century baroque ashlars façade. Inside there is an altarpiece of the same period and a gothic Calvary.

The church of Santo Sepulcro is gothic with a double archivolt door flanked by two rows of apostles, Santiago as a pilgrim, and bishop. The tympanum depicts the Last Supper, the Passion and the Risen Christ appearing to Mary Magdalene. The earlier church was Romanesque. Above it, on higher ground, there once stood a small walled ghetto called Elgacena.

San Pedro de Lizarra is a gothic church situated on the site of the first settlement in Estella. Its tower dates from the seventeenth century.

Santa Maria Jus del Castillo, once known as Santa Maria y Todos los Santos, replaced a Jewish synagogue that stood on this site until 1145. It has a handsome apse with an extraordinary collection of exterior corbels in the elegant and simple Romanesque style of the twelfth and thirteenth centuries. It has a good statue of the Virgin (XIV century). A community of Grandmontinies established themselves here in 1265. It became the parish church in the fourteenth century, and for a time was a royal chapel.

The monastery of Rocamador is simply built with a graceful Romanesque apse. Near the church stood a pilgrim hospital. The image of Nuestra Senora de Rocamador may date from the latter part of the twelfth century.

The twelfth century Romanesque Palacio de los Reyes de Navarre has been restored; it has two original storeys and a third of brick that was added with the two small towers. On the left side of the façade is a capital representing Roland's battle with the giant Farragut. Inside are several rooms used as display or museum space. Nearby in the same plaza the Ayuntamiento, a renaissance edifice on three floors, occupy the building?

The *Casa de Fray Diego* was the palace of the San Cristobal family, a platersque building with a brick façade and a stone doorway. Today it is the Casa de Cultura.

Directions:

The yellow arrows through Estella are very confusing as they take you on (more than one) tour of the town's main "sights". You are advised to obtain a walking tour leaflet from the Tourist Office. Proceed as follows to enter the town and continue your journey.

Turn right along main road but when you enter the town do not follow "centre city" traffic signs over road bridge, (river) but fork right, past sign "Estella" in tiles on a building in front of you. Turn left over a (very) steep humpback bridge. Turn right on the other side to the Plaza San Martin (fountain).

To leave Estella, carry straight on along Calle San Nicolas (i.e. behind Palacio). Keep straight on and pass under archway at end of the street to a road junction (church on your left). Keep straight on this main road, which divides after 300 m. Cross over to the right hand side and take the right fork, up an UMUR next to a petrol station and go up hill behind large hypermarket. Bear right at a factory and keep straight on to village of Ayegui.

Cyclists should leave Estella by the N111 and climb steadily through minor industrial buildings out of the town.

1km to **Ayegui/Irache**
(852)

Some historians date Irache from the Visigoth era. Garcia of Najera founded a pilgrim hospital here (1051-1054). The church of this celebrated Benedictine monastery dates from the twelfth century. So does its Romanesque olive vaulting. The cloister is renaissance and the rest of the building dates from the sixteenth century. This was the time when Irache was a university. Restored in 1942, it is now occupied by Escolapsian Fathers.

On path just before the monastery of Irache, a local 'bodegon' has installed the Fuente del Vino or wine fountain for pilgrims. A wonderful idea but be wary on a hot afternoon.

Accommodation:

Hostel San Andres in the Plaza de Santiago is useful. Accepts bikes; double room with basin, 30 Euros. With bath 4500; add 500 for high season. (T:948-55 07 72) Hostel Cristina at Baja Navarre 1-1 (i.e. go up to first floor) is not cheap, e.g. around 50 Euros for double room. Fonda El Volante, Merkatondoa 2 is well placed for leaving in the morning. A number of restaurants, including El Bordon, La Cepa and Bar/Rest. Casanova (in small street between Plaza de Santiago and main plaza). Solme are not open on Sunday evenings but try the one above the Bar Rochas, Calle Principe de Viana 16.

Tatan HR (T:948-55 02 50), Izarra F (T:948-55 06 78), Maetzu F (T:948-55 04 32), Fonda Joaquin (T:948-55 06 80)

Refuge: Hard to find. Flat in technical college, has bunks and hot water but no kitchen. Ask police or Tourist Office for directions and location map.
Ayuntamiento (T:948-54 63 63)
Campsite: Camping Lizarra, 1.5 km southeast of the town, good facilities, including pool, shop, bar and restaurant (850 pta menu) 1 adult + tent was 8 Euros in 2006.
Cycle Repairs: Vicente Alonzo, Paseo Inmaculada 12, tel. (948)55.07.34.
Directions:
Just before you reach a square (Plaza San Pelayo, houses, flats) at the very top you can either a) turn left for the Monastery of Irache (visible ahead) or b) turn right to miss it. Both Caminos join up again after the Hotel Irache (ahead on the main road).
a) Turn left in square and then right downhill to road. Cross it and veer left up lane to twelfth-century church and Monastery of Irache (500m). Keep straight on ahead up lane. 150 m later, at houses, you again have a choice:
* Keep straight on ahead. This path (way marked but not described here) continues through the countryside to the left hand side of the main road, via Luguin, rejoining the other further on in the village of Urbiola.
** Turn right alongside houses to road opposite hotel. Cross over and behind hotel rejoin option b).
b) At the square (flats, houses) keep straight on ahead down very clear track (you can see it laid out well ahead of you). This takes you out by the Hotel Irache on the main road. After the hotel (i.e. the road to your left), by a complex of chalets, veer right along earth road, cross another and continue ahead to go through tunnel under the road.
This next section is fairly shady and takes you along a gated track through undulating woodland. (conical mountain visible ahead).
Keep straight on clear track. Ignore turns.
When you reach a minor road (at gates) cross it and fork left off road on other side. Veer right on foot path under trees. At end of woods (gate) footpath continues through trees. Join a wide track coming from right and continue to village (visible ahead),

entering by big white house to right of church.
As they leave Irache, cyclists will find the road climbing and dropping over an uninspiring countryside of scrub and wasteland. Few places of interest for another 18 km. Here a well-signed road to the right leaves the N111 and leads to Los Arcos.

Accommodation:
Hotel/Residencia Irache is modern, expensive and has a swimming pool. Hotel Bunkhouse (not a refuge) costs 10 Euros a night. Showers but no kitchen. Not recommended unless you are desperate and have no alternative.

5km **Azqueta**
(857)
Directions:
Continue through village on road (fountain and seats on right hand side) to junction with main road near tunnel (to back left). Fork right downhill to farm and turn left uphill behind last building onto earth track uphill through fields. This becomes a foot path. When you emerge into a field of vines (tip of Villa mayor church spire is visible ahead) veer right along side of the field, uphill, turning left 100m later along field track emerging from field to your right? Pass a restored building that looks like a double-arched church doorway, but is really a medieval fountain and continue to village of Villa mayor.

2km **Villa mayor**
(859)
Villa mayor has a basically Romanesque Church with a very high baroque tower (restored). The processional parish cross dates from the twelfth century and there is a capital representing Roland battling Farragut.
Directions:
Continue to church (Romanesque) and turn left downhill, cutting down path to cut out zigzags. Keep straight for a short distance and turn right along a clear UMUR leaving the one you are on (which leads down to the main road ahead) at right angles.
Walking in the section between Villa mayor and Los Arcos is easy but watch out carefully for way mark. Very pleasant at the

crack of dawn or as the sun fades. Give yourself enough time to reach Los Arcos. There are no villages except Urbiola, no shade, no roads and almost no buildings at all along the way; woods over to the left *and, later, large rock formations ahead to* right. Turn left between two groves of trees, uphill, and continue diagonally through field. Turn right at top on lane by houses, veering left to road at village of Urbiola.

2km Urbiola
(861)
Fountain by church, bar (not always open) 200m back at crossroads to left.
Directions:
Cross over and fork left on concrete road and fork right down earth lane by cemetery (on hill).
(Luquin, the end of the LH variant from Irache, is 500m away on other side of main road, and the two join up here).
Keep straight on, rejoining road by small white house on left. Turn left on UMUR and keep straight on, ignoring turns (first left leads to main road), second right uphill by two buildings on hillside signposted "P.Cazadores". Take third turning (a short cut) on to earth road just before ruined building (a former chapel) on small hilltop to right, returning to UMUR after 200m. 150m later, at top of hill, turn left down earth road (marker stone indicates that you are 5km from Los Arcos...) towards range of small hills, which then turns right 100m later.
After 1.5km, turn left onto track joining from right, just before a ruined chapel on a hill in front of you. 1 km later keep straight on (left) along track coming from back right. Keep straight on, ignoring turnings to Los Arcos (visible only 1.5km beforehand).

10km to Los Arcos
447m, (871)
Village with the ruins of medieval castle. The church of La Asuncion is interesting for its varied decoration and is well worth visiting. It has a plateresque doorway, altarpieces of great size, good fifteenth century paintings and a beautiful

fifteenth century flamboyant gothic processional cloister. Other outstanding features are its handsome renaissance stonework, its elegant tower, and a seated image of the Virgin.

Several houses with armorial devices on facades in the long Call Mayor.

Shop, bank, bars, bar/restaurant, pharmacy. Buses to Estella, Pamplona and Logrono. Fountain.

Accommodation:
Hostel Ezequiel (T:948-64 02 96) recommended. Has bike storage. Special rate for pilgrims. Hotel Monaco (T:948-64 00 00) on the main road is convenient and satisfactory but expensive. Senora Victorina offers rooms for 9 Euros. Bar Mavi c/La Serna 2, menu 10 Euros. Bar Roal, menu 14 Euros..

Refuge: A back of school, basic. Key and 'sello' from the nuns on the side street opposite the church.

Directions:
Enter the town from the north past farm buildings. Turn left at fork and go down the full length of the Calle Mayor till you reach a small triangular "square" at the bottom. Turn right to church (fountain) keep straight on (church on left) through archway ahead. Cross road and then bridge over river Odron,

past public library (right). Keep straight on taking right fork uphill past cemetery (right), Capilla de San Blas (left), electricity substation (left) into open countryside.

From here you will be going more or less parallel *to the road and on a clear day you will have a good view of Sansol 6km away in the distance. There is very little shade in this section but the walking is easy, through fields and vineyards, and is well way marked.*

Ignore turn to left, keep straight on and turn right (just after the track goes into a dip) alongside a banked-up field. Carry on along the bank between 2 fields and when you meet another track crossing diagonally keep straight on (i.e. right fork). Keep straight on along this track, gently downhill into fields. After 1 km, another track coming from the right joins it. Keep straight on. Cross a bridge over stream and keep straight. When you reach a minor road turn left and follow it into village of Sansol.

Cyclists continue straight through the town and the N111 will be regained shortly. This shadeless road continues until Sansol.

6km to **Sansol**
505m (877)

Small hilltop village with few modern buildings. Food shop inside one marked "tabac" in main square.

This village gets its name from San Zoilo, the patron saint of its church. Worth a visit, when open, for its frescoes of the Ascension and Gothic statue of San Pedro. God "aerial view" of Torres Del Rio from the forecourt in front of the church. You can also see the path you have to take to get there. .

Directions:
At entry to village, turn right into Calle Mayor, left into Calle Real, right into next street (uphill), next left, next right, next left and you will come out on the road again. Cross it (N111, KM68, view of Torres del Rio below you now, on a hill top across the river Linares). Turn left and then right down foot path at side of house and go down to minor road below.

Cross over road by bridge, turn right and turn left down footpath to cross bridge over stream (fountain/lavadero left) and go uphill into village of Torres Del Rio.

1km to **Torres Del Rio**
(878)

Another small village with very few modern buildings. Jimeno Galindez gave Irache a monastery in Torres Del Rio in 1190. In the twelfth century, the knights of the Order of the Holy Sepulchre built a singular, octagonal Romanesque church influenced by Byzantine and mudejar. The Christ is a strikingly hieratic and majestic piece. The last prior of the Order, Santiago de Abados, died in 1847.

Refuge: (30) Run by an Italian lady , 10 Euros. Showers, meals and laundry facilities.

Directions:

To continue, fork left at church. Follow road to left then right uphill out of village through orchards, past cemetery (left) to open fields.

This section climbs up and down playing "hide and seek" to avoid the many hairpins bends in the main road. It goes in a fairly straight line, though constantly up and down. (Cyclists try and avoid this road, unless you feel up to it.)

After 1 km descend to crossing with another track. Keep straight on (Olive Groves on right) and pass below the bend in one of the road's many hairpins. Follow track down, then up, fork right to join road at a bend. Continue below road to left on footpath, then above it, for 300/400m and you can then either:

a) Follow yellow arrows and stay on road
b) Avoid a stretch on the road by turning right and up along a bank on its right hand side, parallel to road. Pass through and above a fir plantation.

Both paths meet up again at the Sanctuario de Nuestra Senora del Poyo on right hand side of road. Soon after you come to an ermita (near Bargota). Panoramic views from here, A nice picnic spot.

Turn down to road until next bend (N111 KM72), cross to other side and at end of crash barrier, turn right off road up lane and then left after 20m up small path, following its zigzags to the top of the hill. (You can see Sansol behind you, three trees on hill to right.) Go along lane past building (left) and join road again after 200m. Turn left and after 20m turn right along UMUR, taking right fork (it divides almost immediately). From here you can see both Viana and Logrono in the distance below.

Continue along path, Kso at next fork and follow path as it zigzags down to valley floor. Watch out for the way marks (balises, fleches and yellow tape) as you proceed in a diagonal direction towards Viana. At the bottom, cross olive grove, go up the slope on the other side, and turn left onto a track coming from the right. Continue downhill (track joins from right after approx.200m). Fork left at bottom, then right after 100 m near small white house. 200m later turn left along track coming from the right. (You can see the road over to your left, more or less parallel here). When you reach a wood, bear left diagonally uphill (wood on your right). Keep straight on at top past farm building (left) to road; this is Cornara, the site of a Roman settlement and inhabited until the fourteenth century.

Cross it and turn left into grassy lane. (Now you are setting your sights on a bend in the road near the electric pylons/cables at the top of the hill.) Follow path straight up hill (watching out for way marks) and join road again near (but not going under) cables. Turn left along road. After 100m turn left off road (i.e. road bends to right but you continue more or less in a straight line) along grassy track. Keep straight on. Cross another track and keep straight on till you rejoin road. Continue on road for 1 km, continue on footpath parallel to it for last 500m and enter Viana opposite huge grain silo and by town place name boards.

Cyclists have to leave the N111 if they wish to explore the village. They should return to the N111 before climbing steeply via a series of hairpins over wild, open moorland with little shade or shelter. On reaching the summit, an exhilarating descent leads, 16km later, to a turn to the right into Viana.

9km to **Viana**
(466m)
Attractive small town - the last in Navarre - with cobbled streets and houses bearing coats of arms. Sancho " el Fuerte" founded

this town in 1219 and gave it various privileges. In 1423, Carlos III "el Noble" conferred on it the Pincipality of Viana, the title of the Navarese heirs to the throne. It had a seat on the Council of Navarre. Students of its history are well served by easily accessible documentary sources. Viana had three hospitals in the sixteenth century: San Julian, Santa Catalina, and Nuesta Senora de Gracia.

Roncesvalles held the nomination of las Cuevas until 1810. Aymeric Picaud, with his usual antipathy to all things Navarese, mentions Cuevas, the name of the early settlement: " Further on, a river equally poisonous, flows past a village called Cuevas."

The church of Santa Maria, with the dimensions and architectural richness of a cathedral, was built in the fifteenth and sixteenth centuries and has a magnificent plateresque doorway. In the floor of the atrium facing this amazing door, is a stone slab commemorating Cesar Borgia. There are also the ruins of the sixteenth century church of San Pedro. Viana also has the remains of its wall, many houses with stone coats of arms, and another monument to Cesar Borgia.

All facilities.

Accommodation:
Hostel La Granja (T:948-64 50 78) is at west end of main Calle Navarro Villaslada; double room around 40 Euros. Pilgrim menu for 10 Euros. For cheaper Pension Chavarri (10 Euros per person) telephone first, (Tel:948-64 51 36) . Hostal Casa Armendaria, tel: 948 64 50 07.

Restaurante Borgia may be expensive. Bar La Piedra welcomes pilgrims.

Refuge: new 1993 refuge (40). Albergueria Andres Munoz (50), tel: 948 64 50 78. at the end of the main street turn left San Pedro church. Hot showers, kitchen, dining room and bike storage. 5 Euros. Open April to October.

Directions:
Leave Viana from the Plaza in front of the church by the Calle Navarro Villoslado. Turn right in front of the ruined church of San Pedro (façade interesting), right diagonally then left (Calle San Felices) under arch. Right again (same street name) to the road. Cross it and take the second turn left (down street behind

some seats) and zigzag right to Calle El Rancho. At the bottom, cross the road and turn right by a large school, along a track which veers left past the school's sports ground. Continue along a long brick wall (right) and right again. i.e. going around the boundary of a smallholding. Cross stream and continue left along lane (100m) to a road. Cross it and keep straight on under electric cables to farm (right). Turn left at side of dog-kennel (occupied!) with way mark on it and veer right downhill under embankment to lane coming from left. Take second fork right and keep straight on (left at next fork) until you get to another road. Cross it, take lane opposite and fork right immediately. After a few hundred metres turn left onto wide UMUR signposted *Virgen de Cuevas*. You get a glimpse of Logrono. Ignore next two left turns and veer right below fields until you reach the *Virgen de Cuevas* (once a chapel, it is now a private house in an idyllic setting. It's by a stream, a shaded area with a lot of trees and picnic spots).

20 m later UMUR forks into 3- take path and then fork right 100m later past farm. After 1 km you will see a wood ahead of you near a road; the path leads you to the road which you cross and continue on a foot path under trees on the other side, parallel to the road. The path eventually takes you back to the road, near a paper-packaging factory; cross bridge over a stream (petrol station on left) and leave the province of Navarre to enter La Rioja.

Walk along hard shoulder and on the footpath on right hand side of road marked "Logrono norte" and at N111 K337 (post) cross to left hand side of road. Turn left off it after 10m onto UMUR.

(This is indicated by the first of the many special "Camino" signs you will see, metal notice boards depicting a pilgrim with staff and hat in "penman" format.) Shortly after (10m) you will also see the first of another type of marker – a concrete stele, a little larger than a traditional milestone, with a scallop shell embossed on it. The red and white balises of the French GR system, used simultaneously with the yellow arrows, stop at Logrono for the moment.

Keep straight on along this UMUR, slightly uphill for most of the way, across a road, through fields and vines. (The town of

Oyon is visible away to the right on other side of the road). After 2km the UMUR descends downhill into Logrono, past a warehouse (right) and a few small houses to left and right. At the bottom you reach the main road into the town alongside the river Ebro, passing the cemetery to your right. Cross over; take path behind flats, parallel to river, return to road and cross the stone bridge left over the river into Logrono.

Cyclists will find the descent from Viana to the main road N111. fiine with good views over Logrono and of the route to come. The road is wide with an excellent cycle lane and soon becomes the Logrono by-pass into the city centre.

8km to **Logrono**
(384m)

Large, bustling city and capital of the La Rioja region.

La Rioja region itself corresponds in large part to the ancient province of Logrono and to the valley of the Ebro. It is a land of transition between the Pais Vasco and Navarre, and the meseta of Castile. It is divided into two: the "Rioja Alta", basically vinegrowing, with the city of Haro as its centre, and the "Rioja Baja", more oriented towards market gardening, and centred on Logrono. The Camino de Santiago crosses both parts, passing through beautiful countryside. The gentle and well-cultivated landscape of La Rioja takes the pilgrim into a terrain in which man and nature exist in perfect partnership.

Very early in the ninth century, La Rioja was reconquered from the Arabs. The successful outcome of the famous battle of Clavijo in 844 (when Ramirez I defeated the Moors with the help of Santiago) gave a tremendous stimulus to Christian morale, and by extension, during the following centuries, to the Camino de Santiago.

The territory was soon absorbed into the kingdom of Navarre, with its court at Najera. At the beginning of the eleventh century, Sancho III "el Mayor" encouraged the pilgrimage to Compostela as part of his policy of maintaining good relations with the rest of Europe. Following the battle of Atapuerca in 1054, Fernando I of Castile absorbed the area in accordance with his declared aim of extending his dominions as far as the Ebor. Alfonso VI, another king determined to enhance relations with Europe, also fostered the pilgrimage. The eleventh and twelfth centuries witnessed the construction of outstanding Jacobean monuments in La Rioja.

The wine trade was already well known in the eleventh century, and in the sixteenth, wine was being exported to many parts of Europe. As a result of the pestilence that all but destroyed the French wine trade, intensive cultivation of quality vines began in the nineteenth century.

As one of the market gardens of Spain, La Rioja offers the finest produce: vegetables and fruit. In spring the asparagus is incomparable, together with peppers, artichokes and strawberries. Pickled peppers, known as "guindillas" are a speciality, as is the chacuterie, such as ham cured with garlic and paprika, chorizos and panceta. Beans with pimientos or quail, and in autumn with pigeons, and other dishes prepared in the Riojan style, are typical and filling. The wines of La Riojaare the most famous in Spain!

La Rioja has dances similar to those of Navarre and the Basque country. Noteworthy festivals are the "Procession of Santo Domingo's bread, and the bread of pilgrims" celebrated every 11 May in Santo Domingo de la Calzada. In the fiesta held in Anguiano every 22 July on the occasion of the paternal feast, eight young men dance in procession on stilts some 40cm.high ("la Danza de los Zancos").

A landmark of Logrono is the famous eighteenth century "needle" or singular eight-sided spire of the royal church of Santa Maria del Palacio. The church was founded in the eleventh century and reconstructed in the twelfth in a transitional Romanesque – gothic style. In the sixteenth and seventh centuries it was enlarged and altered again. The main altarpiece (XVI century) is by Arnao of Brussels. The cloister is eighteenth century, although it retains a Romanesque section and a gothic wing dating from the fifteenth century. The image of Nuestra Senora de la Antigua is thirteenth century, but the figure of the Child was added only recently. The whole building is a National Monument.

Near this church stands San Bartolome with its richly sculptured thirteenth century doorway. Its eleventh century tower, showing Mudejar influence, was probably once part of the city wall. The handsome apse in the French style shows similarities with others on the Camino and with Compostela itself. This church has also been declared a National Monument.

The cathedral of Santa Maria la Redonda is in the same part of the city. It owes its name to an ancient polygonal Romanesque church now disappeared. The existing gothic building dates from the fourteenth century. Two graceful towers, known as "La Gemelas" (the twins 1739) flank the façade, a good example of Riojan baroque. Inside, the main altarpiece is also baroque. The chapels contain magnificent grills.

Another National Monument, the church of Santiago el Real, stands in the same street, the Calle Barriocepo. It dates from the beginning of the sixteenth century, with a unique and beautiful nave seventeen metres high. There is a large statue of Santiago Matamoras (XVII century), the work of a Flemish sculptor. The main altarpiece shows a gothic Santiago Peregrino (XIV century), and other scenes from the Apostle's life including the

battle of Clavijo.

The Palace of Espartero is baroque and houses the Provincial Museum, containing worthy historical, artistic and literary artifacts.

Tourist Office is at Calle Miguel Villanueva 10. The chairman of the La Rioja Association of the Amigos de Santiago is Jose Carlos Rodriguez who speaks English well and kindly offers help to cyclists with problems. Tel. 23.05.45.

Accommodation:
Can be difficult at weekends and fiestas. Hotels and resturants are found in the Calle San Juan just north of the main square; try the Sebastian at no.21 (1st floor and can be noisy) (T:941-22 17 79), or La Nuaminte, Calle Sagasta 4. Hotel Isasa (T:941-25 65 99), Calle de los Doctores Castro Viejo 13, Hostel Marques de Vallejo at no.8 in Calle of that name (40 Euros single) (T:941-24 83 33); in the new town Hostel Gonzalo de Berceo in Gran Via del Rey D. Juan Carlos. Also Fonda El Ravellin, next to the Puerto del Camino in centre of the town. Youth Hostel in Calle Caballero de La Rosa 38. Bar/Rest. Casa Salvador, Caballeria 7 has good 800-peseta menu. Casa Juan also recommended for meals.

Refuge: excellent new (60) refuge in rua Vieja near church of Santa Maria del Palacio and bridge. Look for scallop shell on ground. Hot showers (8), kitchen (small), plenty of space for bikes. (Cyclists accepted after 5pm).

Campsite: La Playa, across the river from the city centre, off Avenida de La Playa. Class II site, open 1 June to 30 September.

Cycle Repairs: Ciclos, Avda Colon 6, tel. (941) 23.14.67 and Bicicletas Jose Mary, Calle Duquesa de La Victoria 39, tel. (941) 24.24.14.

Directions:
On the other side of the bridge take the second turn right down the Calle de la Rua Viejo (Refugio on left halfway along), through the old quarter of the town, as its name suggests. At the end, continue along the Calle de Barriocepa to the Fuentes de los Peregrinos in the Plaza Santiago (with its modern checkerboard paving depicting sites along the route to Santiago on both the

Caminos aragones and Frances) and then to the church of Santiago.

Continue along the Calle de Barriocepa to the end, where it bends round to the left. Turn right, right again and then left under an arch in the old town walls. On the other side turn left and then immediately right (Calle de los Depositos) past a roundabout with fountains (and tap) to your left. (Well way marked) Cross a road left and then turn right down Calle del Marques de Murrieta. Continue down this road for some time, past the barracks of the Guardia Civil. After crossing the railway line the road changes its name to Avenida de Burgos.

About 500m after this, fork left (Calle Entrena) behind a petrol station into an industrial estate. Turn left at end, then right between two factories. Veer left diagonally and cross Calle Prado Viejo. Keep straight on other side up tarred lane, which becomes UMUR, leading to dual carriageway after 300m.

Cross (very carefully) and turn R parallel to road onto track and veer left to fork right along gravel Camino (i.e. Not left to factory), lined at intervals with newly planted trees. This is easy to follow and leads after 1.5 km, to some woods and a tarred road just before the Pantano de la Gragera (a reservoir). Continue ahead (left) and then turn right along the wall of the dam. Cross a bridge at the end and turn left under trees to cross FB over stream.

Veer right to pass behind bar and picnic area and then veer left along stony Camino which leads you around the lake (though not along the water's edge). After passing behind the radio/TV mast, turn right at UMUR to cross irrigation channel and 30m later turn left onto tarred lane which becomes UMUR. This veers round to left in a loop (keep straight on (right at fork) uphill before returning you to the main road (view of lake and Logrono to rear). You come to a turn-off to Navarre after passing behind the petrol station and in front of a timber yard. (If raining continue on road as next section may be flooded.)

Take left fork at junction (N120) towards Navarre (up hill ahead of you). After 200m cross road and fork right down a UMUR through vines, fields and over the motorway. To the left are the restored ruins of the old hospital of the Order of San Juan de

Acre, founded in 1185 to look after pilgrims. Follow the track down to a farm immediately below another road. Turn left diagonally up some steps to this road, cross it and follow the street into the village of Navarre.

Cyclists will need to return to the by-pass to leave the city.

As you follow these signs you may be astonished to find you are now on a motorway. Cyclists are allowed on this – just stick to the hard shoulder. Stay on the motorway for 8 km until the N120 (Burgos) is signed on a slip road. Follow this and it will quickly lead you to the turning, to the left, into Navarre. (Do NOT turn onto the A68, as you are not allowed on this motorway with a bicycle.

10km to Navarrete

(909)

Shops, bars, restaurant, bank. Several fountains. Campsite, Fonda.Navarre has two "Calles Mayor", alta and baja (both under restoration), arcaded and lined with casas blasonadas, houses with heraldic devices on their facades. The town also has several alfarerias, pottery factories and workshops producing goods in the dark red clay seen everywhere in the landscape in this region. Monumental sixteenth-century church with a magnificent seventeenth-century Baroque reredos, gilded from floor to ceiling and wall-to-wall.

Directions:

To visit Navarre: turn right up street in front of church and then either:

a) Follow yellow arrows along first street on left (Calle Nueva, roofed-in tunnel effect in first part.)

b) Follow yellow arrows along street on left (Calle Mayor Alta). For a) turn right at end to join option b), at the end of which turn left at end of Calle Mayor into the Calle de Santiago (which becomes the Calle San Antonio after some traffic lights). Turn left down the Calle Arrabal and keep straight on when it is joined by a road coming from the left (it now becomes the Calle San Roque). Continue to a "stop" sign and then along the main road (i.e. straight on). Keep straight on past the cemetery.

This has twelfth-century gates from the former Hospital at the entrance to the village. These were erected when the cemetery was established in 1875. Outside there is a monument to a Belgian woman, Alice de Craemer, who was killed while riding a tandem to Santiago in 1986.

Continue on the main road for 5km, watching carefully for the traffic. Just before the KM16 marker post and a large road bridge ahead there is a turning to the left, way marked with a pin man pilgrim sign. Turn left along it then right down a lane that follows parallel to road. Cross a minor road leading from main road to Ventosa and keep straight on.

[However, to avoid the constant stream of juggernauts, cattle trucks, car transporters, ready-mix concrete lorries, huge vehicles laden with timber, clay, animals, etc, as well as cars and buses doing 100km/h an alternative is available. Turn left 1km approx. after passing the cemetery down a road marked "Sotes 3" and "Hornos3". If you follow this to the village of Sotes and then on to Ventosa you can join the Camino at the main road mentioned above, turning left. *It is not way marked but it is easy to follow and although it is a couple of km longer it is preferable to the perils of the busy main road]*

Keep straight on through fields. 200m after hut (left) – (handy in case of rain) track forks right, more steeply up hill, then forks right after 50m, up a grassy lane. Follow this uphill, then downhill, through vines, past a farm at Alto de San Anton.

5km to **Alto de San Anton**
(914)
Ruins of a convent with pilgrim hospital.
Directions:
Camino meets the main road at a lay-by on a bend. (This is 2km after leaving the main road at KM16.) Turn left, then right to cross road, go through gap in crash barrier, down steps in the embankment and turn left on the track at the bottom. Follow this for 3-4 km, through fields, more or less parallel to the main road all the time. Panoramic views.

Ignore all turnings to left and after passing a stone hut (left) the

track veers round to the right of a round hill (left).
This is the Poyo Roldan, where Roland is reputed to have slain the Syrian giant Ferragut with a huge stone, in the same way that David killed Goliath (from whom the giant is said to have been descended).
When you eventually reach the road at the cement/gravel works turn right and then left after 30m down a UMUR. Veer right past a mountain of sand/gravel and then cross FB over the Rio Yalde (there is another memorial to Alice de Craemer here too). Turn right after FB. Path veers slightly left. Keep straight on along cart track between vines.
After 1 km you reach a huge factory (with a long pilgrim poem painted on its wall, in Castilian with a German translation. Cross canal behind it (Canal Najerilla) and KSSO 400m to minor road. Cross it and keep straight on along cart track until you come to a housing estate, passing a new sports centre (right) and blocks of flats. Keep straight on into street (bar and shop on right) and continue into the centre of town, the road (Avenida de Logrono) veering to the right (and becoming the Calle San Fernando) as it nears the Rio Najerilla in Najera.

10km to **Najera**
(485m),
The town takes its name from the Arabic "place between rocks", a name which will become more obvious as you leave the town along a track which wends its way uphill between high cliffs on either side.

In the eleventh century this was the residence of the kings of Navarre and later of those of Castile. It marked one of the stages on the Camino de Santiago outlined by Aymeric Picaud. Garcia I of Najera (1035-1054) founded the monastery of Santa Maria la Real, and the inn attached to it, to shelter pilgrims. In 1079 Alfonso VI gave the monastery to Cluny, with the object of further promoting the pilgrimage, a measure that did not please the bishop of Najera, who moved his seat to Calahorra.
In the fifteenth century the German pilgrim Koenig described

the hospital of Santa Maria and the other centres of hospitality in the city: " There they give thanks for the love of God in the hospitals and you receive everything you could wish. The meals are very good…"

A visit to Santa Maria La Real is obligatory, to see a great and historic monument of the Camino. The early monastic buildings have disappeared completely and with them the artistic treasure brought together by Garcia I and his wife Estefania.

The church was rebuilt between 1422 and 1453. It has three naves and olive vaulting, save in the crossing, which has star vaulting. The Panteon Real contains numerous tombs, no less than thirty of which are those of princesses. One of the most beautiful belongs to Dona Blanca of Castile (1156), one of the few surviving Romanesque pieces in this area.

The great cloister, also known as the Knight's cloister because of the number of noblemen whose resting place it is, is in the flamboyant gothic style (1517-1528) with abundant and very fine decorative elements. There are also exquisite examples of the plateresque. The choir is one of the high points of Isabel line gothic, executed by sculptors Andres and Nicolas Amutio in 1492, with some Jacobean motifs on the backs of the seats.

In the cloister are represented various scenes of medieval pilgrim life drawn from the twelfth century Cronica Najarense. The image of Santa Maria de Najera (XII century), the chapel of Vera Cruz and the tomb of Lopez de Haro are also worth seeing. Since 1895 the Franciscans have been resident in the monastery.

Accommodation:
Hotel San Fernando, Paseo San Julian 2, (t: 941-36 37 00) serves good, cheap lunch with breakfast at 7.30 AM if requested. Hostel Hispano (good value) near Bar Hispano. Fonda El Moro, Calle de los Martires 21, on west side of river, over bridge, near Santa Maria. Pension Juli, Calle Raure 1-1, and no sign up, so ask. The Palacios restaurants are good value. (T: 941-36 33 20)

Refuge: new refuge near river; cross footbridge, turn left and refuge is at the end on the right. Bunks, hot showers, no kitchen. Refuge (60) in Santa Maria monastery., kitchen, hot showers, bikes are taken in, 5 Euros.

Cycle Repairs: Castrilo Mendoza, San Fernando 42, tel. 36.02.04.

Directions:
On the other side of the river either follow the yellow arrows and turn right and then left, following the signs for the monastery or, a shorter, more direct way, turn left immediately after the bridge down the Calle Mayor (pedestrianised) to the end, into the Plaza Espana and turn right to the church of Santa Maria (set into cliff at rear).

Pass in front of the main entrance (the Calle Costanilla) and keep straight on uphill. Continue on when road becomes a track, trees and woods to either side, up hill or then down (path is in ravine here). Keep left at fork. Keep straight on past farm (left), cross bridge and keep straight on ahead. At fork bear right. Keep straight on. When track crosses another, keep straight on along grassy track. When this eventually reaches a minor road [near tree, for RJ] turn left and continue along it for 1.5km to Azofra.

Cyclists, to get out of Najera, cross back over the bridge and take the first turning to the right, signed as the monasteries route. This is the LR113. It does not look very promising in the first couple of kilometers as the surface is poor and it leaves Najera by way of small, dilapidated industrial units. Soon these are left behind and the road follows close to the river between small market gardens.

7km to **Azofra**
(559m) (931)
On walkers' route
Village with 2 bars, shop, fountain, in main square.
Church of Nuestra Senora de Los Angeles with sculptures of St. Martin of Tours and Santiago as a pilgrim, with staff, cape and hat. Just outside the village on the right is the Fuente de los Romeros, near the site of a twelfth century pilgrim hospital with adjoining cemetery.
Accommodation:
Four star hotel at the Yuso monastery; 100 Euros. Fonda El Comercio in Badaran with rooms at 25 Euros. There is a swimming pool in the village of Berceo.
Directions:
Keep straight on down main street and continue to end of village. Turn right along main road for 50m then left along a farm road (UMUR).
Ignore turns to left or right and keep straight on. After 1km pass a rollo (right), a medieval pilgrim cross. Keep straight on. Turn right into UMUR and then left after 20m. Cross a minor road leading to San Milan de Cogilla and keep straight on, forking left after 10m. Turn left at next junction. Keep straight on.
The original Camino ran in a straight line from Najera to Santo Domingo de la Calzada but today it is interrupted in three places by changes in land ownership. To avoid a long stretch on the main road, an alternative route has now been way marked, if somewhat vaguely, but is not difficult to follow, if as Kipling advised, you keep your wits about you. There are splendid views through undulating fields to the left *of the village of Cirinuela, passing by the edge of Ciruena.*
When you come to another junction, a diagonal crossroads, keep

straight on. Continue for several km. After climbing, the route flattens out (village of Cirinuel plus church and cemetery over to right) and village of Ciruena visible ahead. Keep straight on till you come to it, turn right down road and then left after 300m on to a farm road between fields. Ignore any turns to left or right and continue to Santo Domingo de la Calzada.

Detour to San Millan de La Cogolla

Fifteen kms southwest on the Badaran road are the two monasteries of Suso and Yuso.

The "upper" monastery of Suso is Visigoth in origin and mozarabic in style. The Moorish commander, Almenzor, burned the sanctuary. Inside are items of great archaeological merit, among which is the recumbent Romanesque sculpture of San Milan; there are also the tombs of the seven Princes of Lara and their tutor Nuno Salido, famous in Castilian literature.

The "lower" monastery of Yuso is known as the "Wiscorial of La Rioja". The original Romanesque monastery (1053) is unrecognizable as a result of renovations effected in the sixteenth centuries. The richly decorated church possesses notably fine sculptures in the crossing (XVII century). The cloister, gothic in its lower part and neoclassical above, dates from the mid-sixteenth century, the baroque façade from the eighteenth and so called "escalera del rey" (king's staircase) is neoclassical. There is a large refectory and numerous chapels and altarpieces. The sacristy is baroque and decorated in the rococo style.

The monastery holds the first written record of the Castilian language, by Gonzalo de Berceo, a thirteenth century troubadour and pilgrim. Among its other treasures are the famous caskets of San Milan, and his master, San Felices de Bilibio, precious and outstanding examples of eleventh century ivories. The mortal remains of San Milan (473-574), patron and protector of Castile, also lie here where he passed his long life. The monastic library has an exclusive collection of sixteenth to eighteenth century works, and important codices.

Cyclists should allow at least 4 hours for this detour, one to get there, one to get back and one hour each for the two monasteries. A guided tour is the only way to see Yuso and both are closed on

Mondays.

Accommodation: Refuge *(12) at Yuso with hot showers and kitchen. Badaran has the Fonda El Comerdo with double rooms at 18 Euros and dinner for 10 Euros.*

16km to **Santo Domingo de La Calzada**
(639m)

A pleasant town and well-known pilgrim resting place.

The town takes its name from Santo Domingo (1019-1109), a shepherd. He wanted to enter the monastery of San Milan de Cogilla, but was refused admission because he was illiterate and was in the wrong class. He then built himself a hermitage and chapel in a forest in a notoriously bandit-infested stretch of the Camino between Logrono and Burgos and began to look after the needs of pilgrims. He built a hospital (today converted into a Parador) and church in what became the present-day town, a causeway and bridge over the river Oja. He devoted the rest of his life to road and bridge building. One of his disciples, San Juan de Ortega, continued his work.

The town contains several places of interest. The cathedral occupies the space left by an earlier church consecrated in 1106. The first stone of the church we see today was laid in 1158, but in the sixteenth century it underwent a notable enlargement and renovation. On the basic Romanesque plan and elevation several styles were imposed, the prevailing one being gothic. The oldest surviving part is the apse, with its fine capitals and medallions. The freestanding tower, 69 metres high, is baroque and was put up in 1762. It rivals that of Santa Maria le Redonda in Logrono.

The cathedral had the status of a collegiate church until 1232. Inside there is a museum containing works of art of all styles and periods. The main altarpiece is the masterpiece of Damien Forment (1537-1540), with an alabaster base and walnut panels. Renaissance in style, it contains a variety of profane motifs alongside religious subjects, placed so as to leave as little free space as possible.

The tomb of Santo Domingo, with a reclining statue (XII century), was enriched by the addition of a sumptuous alabaster mausoleum in 1440 and covered by a baldachin executed by Juan de Rasines and Felipe de Bigarney in 1514.

Facing the saint's tomb is the curious hutch containing a white cock and hen, with the words *"Santo Domingo de la Calzada, donde canta la gallina despues de la asada"* ("where the hen clucks after being roasted"). The origin of these words is in the following story: in the tenth century, a youth of eighteen named Hugonell accompanied his parents on a pilgrimage to Compostela. Through the jealousy of a serving-girl at the inn where they stayed, he was accused of theft, tried and hanged, according to the law of the city. His parents heard the voice of their son telling them that he was alive, and that he had been spared through the intercession of Santo Domingo. They hurried to tell the magistrate, who replied that the boy could no more be alive than the roasted cock and hen that he was about to carve at his table. But – a miracle! At that moment the cock and hen jumped from the platter and began to strut and crow in front of the incredulous magistrate! As a memorial, a live cock and hen have been kept in the special cage in the cathedral ever since, and to hear them crow is the hope of every pilgrim.
Inside the cathedral, the chapel of la Magdalena is also outstanding, containing the tomb of its founder, Pedro de

Carranza (XVI century), guarded by a plateresque grille attributed to Cristobal de Andino.

Other sites of interest are the monastery of San Francisco, rebuilt in 1571 by Juan de Herrera; the Cistercian monastery of the Madres Bernardas, built in 1609 by bishop Pedro de Zuniga, and the Hospital del Santo. Today it is a Parador, but was once the ancient pilgrim hospital built by Santo Domingo on the site of a ruined palace. It retains its medieval character.

Accommodation:

Refuge (40) Casa del Santo, kitchen, hot showers, accepts bikes. Opens 1000-2300. Monasterio de la Encarnacion is on the way to town. Hospederia Santa Teresita, Pinar 2, gives 20% pilgrim discount. It is an old peoples home so dinner is early and doors may be locked early. Hostel del Rio, c/Etchegoyen 2. tel: 941 34 02 77. Double rooms for 35 Euros. Hostel El Peregrino, Avda. Calahorra, 15 Euros menu. The Paradorm Plaza dek Santo, 125 Euros. Bar Los Caballeros, 15 Euros menu. El Meson Abuelo Maite, Plaza Almeda, 1000 menu. Casino has a good bar. Restaurant El Rincon de Emilia, p1. Bonifacio Gil and Restaurant El Hidalgo near the Cathedral.

Campsite: Camping Banares, new class I site on N120, 5km before Santo Domingo on the right, with shop, bar and restaurant. Open all year. Ground can be hard for tent pegs. Also the Camping Rioja at Castanares de Rioja, 7km north of the town on the N232 Haro road. Class I site, open all year; recommended, but can be noisy at weekends.

Cycle Repairs: Estenaga, Calle San Roque 47, tel. (941) 34.22.07.

Directions:

Enter town past farm/factory, continue along farm road, when it bends to right to join road. Turn left to crossroads (with rollo), cross over and take right fork past flats and then keep straight on down Calle Mayor (fountain). Pass cathedral and keep straight on. Turn left at end of Calle Mayor and then right into Calle de los Palmarejos and keep straight on when it continues as Avenida de la Rioja. Cross the bridge over the Rio Oja (ermita, 1917, at entrance to bridge).

After crossing the bridge and causeway walk along the main

road for 6km. Turn off it left uphill between KM49 and KM50 and then immediately right uphill into the village of Granon.

6km to **Granon**
(724m)
Shop, bar, pharmacy.
In the Middle Ages Granon was a walled city with an important castle. In the eleventh century it had two monasteries, Santo Tome and San Miguel. It also had a pilgrim hospital that survived, though in a poor state, until the nineteenth century. Today its parish church contains a good altarpiece by Forment and Beogrant. The hermitage of the Jews is a sixteenth century cruciform edifice. The basilica of Nuestra Senora de Carrasquedo, patroness of the town, is splendid.
Accommodation.
Refuge : (26) in church with kitchen and hot baths. Moderately clean. There are evening prayers for pilgrims. Bikes are accepted
Dinner and breakfast provided.
Directions:
Cross road on entering village, go up short flight of steps and walk along main street past church (left). Continue a little further and then turn right. (way marked). At first it may seem as though you are going back, but you then turn left by a modern barn building onto a minor road. Follow road round a bend after 200m (i.e. do not go straight on) to barn with yellow arrow on it. Cross bridge over river Relachigo and take second left along farm road. Fork right after approx. 1 km (village of Recedilla del Camino visible ahead) and follow track 1.5km to village. Just before you reach it turn right at farm to join road. Pass another Rollo and fountain (right).

3.5km to **Redecilla del Camino**
(956.5)
Between Granon and Recedilla you pass from La Rioja into the province of Burgos.
The handsome church contains a valuable Romanesque baptismal font, often reproduced in volumes on Romanesque

art, and carved with towers and buildings as a symbol of the celestial city. In the south door is an attractive stone statue of the Virgin (XVI century).

In this area there were a number of hospitable institutions for the relief of pilgrims, such as those of Santa Pia or Santa Cristina, and another near the river Relachico, founded by San Milan in the twelfth century. In front of the church stands the ancient hospital of San Lazaro.

There are also a few houses with coats of arms.

Accommodation:.

Refuge:(24) Opposite the church. Two dormitories, two bathrooms and a kitchen. Shop and panaderia on main road. Bar.

Directions:

Continue along main street at church (fountain) and public garden (fountain). Keep straight on to end of village and join road again (KM55) on leaving village). Continue on main road, cross bridge over river Relachilo (be careful, the bridge is on a sharp bend).

2km to **Castildelgado**

(958.5)

Petrol station, bar/restaurant El Caserio (has rooms), hostel restaurant El Chocolateria. Church.

Accommodarion:

Hotel El Chocalatero, 45 Euros. double, 27 Euros single. Fonda El Caserio which is a better option but closes in October.

Directions:

Keep straight on along main road. 2km later turn left up minor road to Viloria de la Rioja (where the Camino does a "C" shaped "loop" to take you through the village which was the birthplace of Santo Domingo de la Calzada), before returning you to the main road again. Keep straight on.

5.5km to **Villamayor Del Rio**

(964)

Bar/restaurant. You may be able to get a room.

Fountain. (This is not a "big town on a river" but " a small village by a stream").

Directions:
Stay straight on main road until just after K64. Turn right off road by warehouse, down lane leading, after 1km, to church of Santa Maria in Belorado.

6km to **Belorado**
(760m)(970)
Pleasant small town with tree-lined main square. You can buy food here. Most unusually, there is a church for winter attendance and a church for the summer.
The town received a charter in the eleventh century from Alfonso I of Aragon. The church of Santa Maria is a sixteenth century refurbishment of its older predecessor, the church of the Virgen de la Capilla. Some of the tombs are of historical and religious interest. A chapel dedicated to Santiago, has a sixteenth century altarpiece. The 17th century church of San Pedro in the plaza Mayor deserves a visit.
The monastery of San Francisco came into existence in 1250. It was reconstructed in the sixteenth century. St Bernard of Siena stayed here on his way to Compostela. The hospitals of San Lazaro and La Misericordia, close to the hermitage of Nuestra Senora de Belen, were generous havens for pilgrims for many centuries. The ruins of the medieval castle tell a fascinating story. Do visit the nearby caves, the dwelling place of impoverished but intelligent hermits for many years.
Accommodation:
Refuge:(22) near Santa Maria. Hot water and kitchen. Open from 15 May to 15 September. Hotel Belorado tel 947 58 06 84. -Tariff. 50 Euros. Storage for bikes. Hostal Ojarre tel: 947 58 03 90. Tariff. 45 Euros. Hostal Toni, Avda. de Cerezo de Rio Tiron. 40 Euros.
Directions:
To leave Belorado, turn left (church on right), left again, right to arcaded main square. Cross it in a straight line (trees, bandstand) and go down the Calle Jose Antonio de Ribera. Turn left. Either turn left again, then right to main road or keep straight on behind blocks of flats, joining road at a sawmill. Turn right and proceed straight. Cross the river Tiron, pass

petrol station (left after approx.1km out of Belorado). 20m later, (before KM68) you come to a turning to the left, down a minor road, signposted "San Miguel de Pedroso 3". Turn left and immediately right off it onto a track. Turn right again almost immediately and the lane is parallel to main road. It remains so to Espinosa del Camino.

Go straight on and be alert for way marks. Cross a track and keep straight on along a grassy footpath, joining a track from behind left and then another to side left. Keep straight and after 200m you reach the village of Tosantos.

3km to Tosantos
(818m)(973)

Bar 100m on main road. Cemetery uphill to left. Twelfth century Ermita Virgen de la Pena set in hillside on the right, on other side of main road.
Directions:
Do not go as far as the main road; fork left up a farm road. This takes you to the village of Villambistia.

2km Villambistia
(975)
Directions:
Fork right just before church (right). Keep straight on, cross bridge over river; pass fountain (right) and chapel of San Roque. Keep straight on (i.e. do not follow road round to right). The village has a forlorn air. The main road is to the right, more or less parallel to Camino.

Don't deviate until you reach the road. Turn left and 20m later turn right into a lane and into village of Esoinosa del Camino.

1.5km Espinosa del Camino
(976.5)
There is a bar here which sells food and canned drinks.
Directions:
Go straight past the fountain (right). Follow road round to

right. Turn left behind the last line of houses onto a farm road. Go straight on, ignoring next 3 turns to right. After you pass the Abside de San Felices (ruins of the medieval monastery of San Felix de Oca, right) a UMUR leads round to the left (view of Villafranca Montes de Oca ahead, with its large, prominent church).

Continue towards road. Turn right and follow it to the village of Villafranca Montes de Oca.

7km to **Villafranca Montes de Oca**
(948m), (981)

This is referred to as the "Town of the Franks", because like others along the Camino, the village owes some of its prosperity to the pioneering Frankish settlers and astute traders who catered for the needs of the pilgrims in the Middle Ages.

Oca, the seat of a bishop from apostolic times, passed to Burgos in 1075. Its first bishop was San Indalecio, a disciple of Santiago. San Indalecio has an honoured place in the chapel of the Virgen de Oca, which also has a twelfth century statue. On his feast day –11 June – a pilgrimage is made to the site reputed to be the scene of his martyrdom. It is claimed that a spring erupted here.

The parish church (XVII century) was built on the site of an earlier church, which in turn, was erected over the ruins of the cathedral burned down by the Arab forces when they besieged Cerezo.

A statue of Santiago with a reliquary in its chest is venerated in the church. A scallop shell brought from the Philippines serves as a holy water stoup.

Higher up stands the hospital of San Antonio Abad. Dona Juana, wife of Enrique II, founded it in 1380. Its archives reveal that in the sixteenth century it sheltered 18,000 pilgrims a year. This is a quite remarkable figure. Two centuries later, it had only 36 beds. It had a doctor and administrators. Kunig (**German U**) praised it warmly: " Remember the Queen's hospital, which provides such good meals to the brothers." Laffi was also similarly appreciative: " They are very kind to the pilgrims, particularly in the hospital where they eat very well".

Accomodation:

Refuge: (18) in a restored hospital in San Antonio. Keys from Mr. Pedro Zamora, on main street, number 39. Hostel El Pajaro, tel: 947 58 20 29. Rooms are for 35 Euros. No bath, bikes are accepted. Good meals. Breakfast from 0700. Bakery and Pharmacy which supply sello. Bar el Puerto has a shop.

Directions:

On the main street, turn off the right side of the church (left). Pass ruins of Hospital San Antonio (right) and continue uphill beside long modern wall. Pass trees and join farm road from left. Turn right. Good views to rear on a clear day.

Fork right shortly afterwards to join another track from right at a crossroads. Keep straight on. Go straight up hill and after 2km you reach the signposted Fuente de Mojapan (literally "moisten bread"), a popular pilgrim-resting place in former times in an area too menacing to cross at night. Robbers apart there were wolves to contend with.

The track leads to the woods (semi-shaded) and veers to left. Keep straight on, ignoring paths to left and right. Join forest road coming from left and keep straight until you reach the memorial to the fallen in the Civil War (right) the Monumento de los Caidos, (alt.1163m) There's a steep descent to the Peroja river. Cross the Peroja and climb again.

(The path is in a dead straight lane here. It is visible from the monument, and is parallel *to main road.)*

Path veers left and shortly after, near road forks right. 500m onwards, a wide forest track emerges. Turn right onto it at MP57 (signposted). Trees obscure RJ way marks and MP57. Flashes/yellow paint on pile of stones is visible at night. Turn left to small unmarked opening in embankment to footpath. This is about 100m after Council of Europe way marking on right.

At the major crossing (MP61) and trig point type pillar, keep straight unless you want to visit the Fuente del Carnero, way marked 200m to left.

(Fuente signposted in yellow. This is at the side of the road, by the Ermita de Valdefuentes, the sad remains of an old pilgrim hospital.)

After a kilometre or so, join road coming from left [RJ fork left}. About the same distance later, a similar track merges from behind right. A very large wooden cross is way marked. Keep straight on.

After a further 2km the church of San Juan de Ortega ("St. John of the Nettles") is fleetingly visible in the distance through the trees to the left. Turn left at next fork. Track opens out about 500m later and goes downhill. Another 500m and you reach the church of San Juan de Ortega.

13km to **San Juan de Ortega**
(1040m)

In the twelfth century, San Juan De Ortega, the famous pupil of Santo Domingo de la Calzada – with whom he teamed up in constructing the bridges of Logrono, Najera and Santo Domingo – founded a monastery and pilgrim hospital in the spot that bears his name. He was most solicitous of their safety and welfare, well aware of the perils faced by the pilgrims in the region. They were frequently assaulted and robbed: "Die ac nocte jacobipetas interficientes et multos expoliantes". Because of his good work for the pilgrims and the high esteem in which this noble man was held by society, the Holy See granted him its protection, and kings and nobles conferred on him numerous honours and privileges.

San Juan died in Najera and is buried in Ortega. His compassionate will of 1152 provided for the enduring structure that up to this day helps pilgrims on their way to Compostela :"in servito pauperum in via sancti jacobi...."

Until 1431, the canons regular, founded by San Juan de Ortega, looked after the sanctuary and hospital. In 1853, the monks of the Hieronymite order replaced them. Laffi (1670) said that the latter were rich, and claimed that they did much charitable work for the pilgrims: "Questi Padri sono molto richi e fanno molto carita alli pellegrini".

With the misappropriation, the monastic life disappeared from this historic spot. The properties were confiscated and the buildings and infrastructure began to decay. Restoration work started in 1694, and San Juan de Ortega entered a new and more hopeful phase.

The building of the monastery church began in 1152 and was completed many years later. The transverse nave and the three apses are Romanesque. In the fifteenth century, the church was enlarged. When the existing façade was incorporated, the building was complete. The apsidal windows are works of great beauty. Their unostentatious but singular form, and the striking scenes from the childhood of Jesus Christ, especially the Annunciation, are enduring works of art.

The mausoleum, with its sepulcher and baldachin, is flamboyant gothic. It was commissioned by Pedro Fernando de Velasco and Dona Mencia de Mendoza (1464). Some scenes from the life of San Juan are depicted on the sides of the tomb. As a man who cared deeply about pilgrims, it is most appropriate that San Juan is shown seen receiving pilgrims. Legend records that he requests his nephew Martin to give the pilgrims food. A perplexed Martin truthfully replied that no bread was available. The saint firmly ordered his nephew to go to the bread barrel, which to his amazement, Martin found bursting with loaves of freshly baked bread!

A Romanesque sepulchre, a work of consummate artistry, has been in the crypt since 1966. It was intended as a repository for the saint's earthly remains but little came of this loving but ambitious project.

The final addition to this spiritual complex was the church of San Nicolas, which Isabel I of Castile commissioned in 1477. It has some good altarpieces and grilles, and a hospederia. With its sixteenth century patio it is today a refuge for pilgrims.

Accommodation:
Refuge (60) at the monastery. Volunteers from the Amigos de Santiago of San Sebastian act as wardens in the summer. Rooms for family and group use. No kitchen, but good washing facilities. Get your own food from the local version of the take-away if there is one! Sometimes you may share a meal after Mass, with garlic soup and discussion hosted by the priest. Notice on door: Open at 15.30 for walkers and 19.30 for cyclists.

Directions:
Pass the church and the road waits. Cross and enter woods. You can not or should not miss very large wooden cross (some 15-20ft high) and cledo shortly after. Proceed straight along forest road. Pass another large cross and another cledo. Go straight. Road opens out, cross a ravine (path banked up across it). Keep straight on and fork right at third large cross descending towards village of Ages.

4km to **Ages**
Directions:
Path joins main street. Follow this past fountain (right) and follow street through village. Continue to Atapuerca.

2.5km to **Atapuerca**
(1000.5)
Two fountains, bar panaderia. Fortress-like church up hill.

Archaeological excavations nearby have recently unearthed a spectacular fossil, "Atapuerca man".

Accommodation:

Refuge (16) at c/Iglesia 9. Hot bath and kitchen 8 Euros. Key from nearest bar.

Directions:

Turn left just before bar (right), diagonally off road, and turn right towards the TV antenna (be alert for way marks). The path divides. Fork left and follow track which veers left leading into the village of Cardenuela.

5.5km to **Cardenuela**
(1006)

Directions:

Turn right along road, keep straight through village and continue on road. Ignore turns to left and right to Orbaneja.

2km to **Orbaneja**
(1008)

Directions:

Go straight. Cross motorway. Exercise due care. Pedestrians are warned not to take unnecessary risks. Stay alive should be the prudent motto!

You have a choice between continuing to Villafria and along the main road into Burgos (option A. Or turn left *and take a slightly longer, no more "scenic" but quieter and a lot safer, route, to enter the town from the northeast instead via the suburb of Castanares and the N120 (option B).*

A. Road Option via Villafria :

Cross the motorway and stick to road for 2km until you reach the railway line (Madrid-Irun), parallel to the motorway. Follow road round (rubbish tip on left), cross bridge over railway. Either follow road till it joins the N1 after 100m, or turn right at bend in road immediately after bridge and go down lane to church of Villafria.

4km **Villafria**
(1012)
Villafria is a suburb of Burgos. Two bars close to the church. Assertive, confident storks have ingeniously appropriated the church tower. It is their domain and hardly any one complains. You will find a fairly well stocked shop. Some bars on main road. Also a hostel and bar with rooms and restaurant. Frequent bus service to Burgos Monday to Saturday, but never on a Sunday!

Directions:
Continue on N1 into Burgos. A nightmare stretch of 7km taken over by heavy lorries, fast cars and buses. To say this is the worst section of the whole Camino is to be guilty of an understatement. Exercise maximum care. A moment of carelessness can be life threatening. We do not exaggerate, watch out, for as the English say, better late than dead on time. Keep straight on the main road towards the city centre. 4-5km you arrive at a large crossing and your road becomes the Calle Vitoria. At another large junction (traffic divides right for Santander, centre for city and left to Madrid) you can either continue along the Calle Vitoria into the centre of Burgos or take a road parallel to it on the left, along the river and the shaded Avenida General Sanjurio. This becomes the pedestrianised Paseo de Espolon in the city centre.

Alternatively, if you have not yet picked up the yellow arrows again turn right at the large junction along the Avenida del General Vigon and left along the Calle de las Calzadas. Follow the way marked route described below under Castanares.

B.Alternative route via Castanares:
On crossing the motorway (exercise maximum care), turn left 50-60m later down UMUR beside military barracks and right (passing behind it) 30m later. Continue through fields, parallel to motorway on your left for a while.

This is the alternative to the commonly used entry to Burgos along the N1. It is no less interesting, simply much quieter and far less menacing. Look out for the way marks. With little suitable space for their insertion, they are often on the ground. If they escape your otherwise sharp attention, you are likely to head towards two large factories against a silhouette of chimneys, one of them red and white and probably emitting smoke. The spire of Burgos cathedral may be visible behind them to their left.

[RJ: Head for the TV antennae and the motorway. Ignore right turn and go straight on. Fields give way to waste ground. Cross another track about a kilometre later and stick to the road. Keep straight on after second crossing a few yards later. Track then veers left towards Castanares (factories, water tower, suburb on the N120). Cross bridge over stream, go under HT cables and enter Castanares.

3km to **Castanares**
Fountain, 2 bars/restaurants on main road.
Directions:
Turn right at fountain, parallel to main road, and then right again on track parallel to road (and beside it). Cross road carefully by bar/restaurant 20m later and go under road bridge (N111 Madrid-Bilbao road) after (also carefully) crossing slip road (just after road KM107) and continue on hard shoulder. 200 m later turn left and then right down track parallel to road towards a large block of flats, passing to the left of them (factory on your left) down ex-tarred road (the Calle Mayor de Villauda), which becomes a residential street (shop, bar). At end keep straight on UMUR alongside field (red and white chimney is now to your right), parallel to N120 all the time.
At last factory, go under railway line, go up flight of steps, turn left and then immediately right down more steps behind block of flats (i.e. to the left of it, the Calle Villafranca).
At the end of the street (fountain, bar and sports ground to right) keep straight on ahead down alley between walls and then left at end, then right down street with municipal sports centre on left.
At end of street (Plaza de Toros on left, football stadium ahead) turn right, cross road and keep straight on ahead alongside to right of football ground (i.e. a "staggered" turn).
Pass Red Cross HQ; park (left, fountain). The two "caminos" merge here, i.e. the variant with the road route via Villafria.

Cross over and go down street (Calle Maestro Justo del Rio) beside Guardia Civil barracks (right) and Hotel Puerta de Burgos (left). Cross waste ground diagonally. Cross Avenida General Vigon and continue ahead down Calle de las Calzadas to Plaza San Juan at end (Museo Municipal on left near end).

Cross bridge over a river, go under arch and continue down Calle San Juan, cross Avenida del Cid Comprador. Keep straight, Calle San Juan, then Calle de Avellanos and Calle Fernando Gonzalez to the cathedral.

7km to **Burgos**
(856m) (1019)

Burgos is a beautiful city with wide tree-lined streets, a fascinating old quarter and a series of canals and rivers. It has a refuge, hotels, hostels, Fondas and tourist office (in the Calle de San Carlos) as well as full range of shops including cycle repairs, supermarkets, bars, restaurants and banks.

Originally Burgos was a fortress situated in the pass between the meseta and the Cordillera Cantabrica. It was founded by a count Diego in 884. Fernando Gonzalez raised it to the status of "caput Castelliae" ("chief castle"). In 920 it was referred to as a "city". Kings Fernando I and Alfonso VI stimulated its growth. Burgos became the capital of the then recently created kingdom of Castile (1035). By the end of the thirteenth century it was a strongly fortified city. It had eleven gates, five of which survive. The most outstanding are San Esteban and San Martin, in the Mudejar style, together with Santa Maria, which resembles a triumphal arch, rebuilt in 1534.

Trade and commerce gave Burgos a special status in the thirteenth and fourteenth centuries. It hit a bad patch later and was reduced to penury. This was to change dramatically. The twentieth century recalled it to life. There was spectacular industrial development with a population to match. At the last census, there were 170, 000 people. This city with a wonderful history and an impressive artistic inheritance attracts many tourists from Europe and America.

The cathedral, built on a grand scale, is one of Spain's most beautiful aesthetic and architectural creations. It has been described as a 'monument to the Divine.' It stands on the site of a former Romanesque church built by Alfonso VI in 1092.

Fernando III "el Santo" and Beatriz of Swabia, daughter of the German Emperor, tied the knot in this cathedral. With the encouragement and support of Ferdinand, bishop Mauricio began work on a new church. He laid one of its foundation stones in 1221. It was completed several centuries later. Different architectural styles preserved the original harmony of the initial gothic. The first master builders were French.

Eight sculptured pinnacles crown the cupola, nearly fifty metres high. The two towers have pinnacles of white stone, an octagonal pyramid about twenty-eight metres in height. This is the work of Juan de Colonia (1445-1458). The north façade or Coroneria contains some very appealing sculpture; on the north side, on a lower level, is the plateresque Puerta de la Pellejeria, the work of Francisco de Colonia (1516). On the south side is the Puerto del Sarmental, adorned with some brilliantly executed sculptures of the twelve apostles in the lintel, and angels and the elders of the Apocalypse on the archivolts; the tympanum depicts Christ Pantocrator with the evangelists in the act of writing. Above is an imposing rose window bordered by three rows of arches.

The main façade of Santa Maria has three doors, leading to the cathedral's three naves. The lower part was replaced by the existing classical façade in the 18th century. Only four small statues on either side of the central door have survived. The central part of the façade has an openwork balustrade with a rose window. The upper part has two arcades.

A Latin cross dominates the ground plan. The central nave is twice the width of the side aisles with single transepts, ambulatory and apsidal chapels. The floor is covered by Carrara marble (1864). The choir occupies the same comfortable and hallowed enclosure since the dawn of the seventeenth century. Seats of boxwood and walnut, carved by Felipe de Bigarny (1507-1512), make for an unusually pleasant singing ambience. The reclining statue of bishop Mauricio, wood covered with glided copper (1260), is also worthy of your attention.

A word about the tomb of El Cid and his wife Dona Gimena. The vault, in the form of an eight-pointed star, has been strongly influenced by the Arab aesthetic school. It is the respected work of Juan de Vallejo (XVI century). Pillars decorated by gothic and plateresque motifs support the vault. The large monumental altarpiece is of gilded walnut, the work of several sculptors (1562-1578). Behind the altar are some fine sculptures by Felipe de Bigarny (1499-1513) and Alonso de los Rios (1679).

Pedro Fernandez ordered the Capilla del Condestable De Velasco, Constable of Castile's family burial chapel, is a wonderful example of the flamboyant gothic style. The vault forms an eight-pointed star, the stained glass is Flemish in origin and the splendid large windows of the upper level are gothic. Work on the chapel began in 1482 and was completed in 1494, but the loving task of embellishing it continued until 1526. The central altarpiece is by Bigarny. Make up your own mind about its merits. The tomb of the Constable and his wife, in apparently tranquil repose at the foot of the high altar, is also said to be the work of Bigarny. A 34-ton block of jasper marble, intended for the tomb of Don Pedro's grandchildren, is a poignant reminder of good intentions frustrated by circumstances. The exceptionally fine ironwork by Cristobal de Andino around the tomb (1523) commands respect.

Take your time, and you will not be disappointed by The Escalera Dorado ("Golden Staircase") in the renaissance style by Diego de Silo (1519-1526). A thirteenth century doorway gives onto the square gothic cloister, which has a gallery, hence two levels. The chapter house and three other gothic chapels open on the cloister and house the cathedral museum. This has some valuable items of considerable historic and artistic interest - sculpture, paintings, codices, metalwork and much more. Besides these chapels, there are thirteen others of different styles and degrees of interest: the baroque altarpiece of the chapel of Santa Tecla (XVIII century), the gothic ones in those of Santa Ana and La Trinidad (XVI century) and many gothic and renaissance tombs sculpted by masters of the art are also worth seeing.

The chapel of Santiago, which obviously has most relevance to the Camino, occupies one of the best positions in the cathedral, in the ambulatory. The mounted figure of the Apostle appears on the upper part of the entrance grille, and in the altarpiece.

Jacobean influence appears in many other details. In the choir, one of the seats represents the Virgin's appearance to Santiago at the Pillar in Zaragoza. In the cloister, one of the capitals shows the head of a pilgrim. The museum contains a good statue of Santiago.

You should visit the Santo Cristo of Burgos (XIII century). It once belonged to the Augustinian monastery. With the misappropriation of 1835 it passed to the cathedral. The image is the subject of many traditions and legends.

In that part of the city outside the walls, but today still in the centre, stand the early church of San Juan, now that of San Lesmes. In his struggle against the kings of Navarre, Juan 1 ordered it separated a little from the wall for greater security. The existing gothic church is fifteenth century, heavily restored in the sixteenth and in 1968. On the last occasion, the tomb of San Lesmes was opened and the saint's remains were seen. The sepulchre, situated in the lower part of the church, came to occupy the centre of the presbytery above. The restored church, work on which was commissioned by the local authorities and French pilgrims from Loudon, was opened on 30 January 1969.

Facing the church in the eleventh century was the hospital that Alfonso VI placed under the protection of the Benedictine abbey of Chaise-Dieu in the Haut-Loire; San Lesmes, as prior, not only contributed to the improvement and growth of the city – he was an architect and builder – but also to improving the Camino de Santiago.

The church has beautiful altarpieces and contemporary painted panels of the Castillian School. On the right of the entrance is the tomb of Diego de Carrion, with the figure of Santiago in relief. It is impossible to describe in detail all the important monuments in Burgos; a brief resume must suffice.

San Nicolas, (XV century) has a magnificent altarpiece by Francisco de San Esteban, reconstructed between 1280 and 1350. Its sculpture is reminiscent of the cathedral's Puerto de la Coroneria, and contains notable renaissance tombs, tapestries and paintings of the Castilian school. San Gil has many tombs, all of artistic merit. That of Juan Garcia of Burgos, executed by Diego de Siloe and situated in the sacristy, is outstanding. Santa Agueda was where Alfonso VI swore before Roderigo Diaz de Vivar (El Cid) that he had not been involved in the death of his brother, don Sancho.

The Casa del Cordon or Palace of the Constables of Castile is plateresque, the work of Simon de Colonia, and restored at the beginning of the present century by Vicente Lamperez who added the large towers. It was a royal residence. Felipe "el Hermoso" (Philip the Fair) died here; Juana "la Loca" (Joan the Mad) stayed here, as did Carlos I (the Emperor Charles V) on his way to Yuste, and Francois I (Francis I) of France, taken prisoner at Pavia.

The Casa de Miranda is a palace built in the plateresque style in 1545 for canon Francisco de Miranda. Since 1955 it has housed the Provincial Archaeological Museum, which contains important metalwork and paintings. The Casa del Angulo has a graceful plateresque doorway.

The hospitals, of which Burgos had a great number (fifteen were of notable standing), also merit your attention. Alfonso VIII founded one of the most famous, the Hospital del Rey. The part of it that remains dates from the sixteenth century and is plateresque in style. This beneficent institution continued to minister to pilgrims until the nineteenth century, as a dependency of Las Huelgas. It passed into royal custody, then into that of the Diputacion Provincial (provincial council). It now houses a university faculty. The Puerto del Romero (1526) and numerous sculptures with Jacobean motifs in the baroque church make it of great interest.

Accommodation:

Accommodation is very difficult to find in fiesta time (late June), in July and at weekends. If planning to stay here try to arrive as early as possible in the day.

Hostel Conde Miranda (T: 947-26 52 67) above the bus station is clean and comfortable. Pension Ansa, Calle Miranda 9-1, opposite the bus station, has bike storage (double room 27 Euros); Hotel Espana (T: 947-20 63 40), Paseo del Espalion 32, also looks after bikes. Hostel Hidalgo (T: 947-20 34 81), near Tourist Office, Almirante Bonifaz 14-2 is reportedly shabby but clean and cheap. Hostel San Juan, Bernabe Perez Ortiz 1 (corner of Calle Vitoria) did doubles in 1993 for 30 Euros. Hotel Norte y Londres (T: 947-26 41 25), Plaza Alonso Martinez 10 is noisy at the front, but otherwise good and bikes are looked after. Hostel Victoria (T: 947-20 15 42), Calle San Juan 3, is cheap and may feel so. Hostel Manjdn, Calle Conde Jornada 1-7, is good value, clean and comfortable (no meals), located near river, 200 yards from statue of El Cid. More expensive hotels include the El Cordon, Almirante Bonitaz and Condestable. Restaurant Rincon de Espana between the river and the cathedral, is recommended. Also the Gaona, adjacent to south side of cathedral, Calle Virgen de La Paloma and the Restaurant Flor, Calle Avellanos. More expensive (with 1700 pta set menu) but very good is the Arancha, Calle Gasset 4 (near the Hostel Manjon). Pension Arribas is cheap. Hostal San Juan, Berbabe Perez Oriz 1, tel: 947 20 51 34. Room from 55 Euros. Hotel Notre y Londres, Plaza Alonso Martinez 10 has rooms for 45 Euros. bikes are accepted. Meson El Cid, tel: 947 20 87 15. Youth Hostel: Resedencia Juvenil Gil de Siloe, YHA card is required Meals. Available from July to September.

Refuge: In July 1993, a large refuge was opened near the monastery of Las Huelgas, with good facilities but no kitchen. Plenty of space for bikes. An autumn 1993 pilgrim described the refuge he stayed in as a 'barrack-like set of huts in a large park, with outside cold showers, and medieval music at 7am'. For 1994 ask at the Tourist Office.

Campsite: Fuentes Blancas, 4km from centre on the road to the Cartuja de Miraflores and San Pedro de Cardena; class I site, open 1 April to 30 September. Good if expensive restaurant. Only 400 yards from the Cartuja (see below). Also campsite at Cabia, 12km south-west on road to Valladolid; has swimming pool and bar, but no shop. Noisy.

Cycle Repairs: Ciclos Cano, calle del Carmen 7, tel. (947)20.71.27. Ciclos Gardia, Pasaje Isaac Albeniz 2, tel. (947)23.88.87. Luis Velasco, Calle Barantes 3, between Cathedral and Plaza Castille reported helpful.

Directions:

To leave Burgos, either turn left at the end of the Calle Vitoria to the Paseo de Espolon if you have not already done so and continue along the river on the Avenida del Generalissimo, the Paseo de la Isla, the Paseo Fuente. Cross the river by the Puente Malatos (the last one before the railway bridge).

Alternatively, from the cathedral (with the church of San Nicolas to your right) continue along Calle Fernando Gonzalez, passing seminary (on your right), and go under archway at end. Turn left immediately down flight of steps, cross road and keep straight on ahead down Calle del Emperador, pass church of San Pedro de la Fuente (left, fountain) and turn left at the bottom into Calle Vilalon. Continue to end, bringing you to the river Arlanzon, and cross it by the Puente Malatos.

Turn right on the other side along the main road past the Hospital del Rey (now restored as part of the University's Law Faculty). Weighbridge (bascule municipal).

After 3km, at traffic lights opposite the Meson Restaurante Bellavista, the main road veers left. Fork right down a minor road (tree lined). At the end (0.5km) keep straight on along a farm track (parallel to railway line to left) past fields, a tree plantation and more fields. Keep straight on ignoring turns to left and right. After 3km reach Villabilla de Burgos.

For cyclists, finding the well signed N120 out of Burgos should be no problem. There is even a special cycle track.

Monastery of las Huelgas :

This was a palace and a royal pantheon as well as a monastery. It owes its name to its use as a royal summer retreat. Founded by Alfonso VIII in 1187 at the request of his wife, Eleonor Plantagenet, it soon became the residence of the royal children and the daughters of noblemen.

The Abbess of Las Huelgas was custodian and controller of 75 towns, and this Cistercian monastery was chief of twelve such institutions. It coined its own currency, and collected taxes and issued licences to celebrate Mass. These privileges were abolished in 1873 by Pope Pius IX.

Tournaments were celebrated here, kings crowned, and knights created by monarchs Ferdinand III "el Santo", Edward III of

England, Pedro I, Enrique II and Juan II. A statue of Santiago figured prominently in this ceremony; it had moveable arms which enabled it to hold the sword. It has been preserved and can be seen in the chapel of Santiago.

The group of buildings is partly surrounded by a wall with battlements. The church, with Romanesque and gothic features, has three naves, a crossing and five apsidal chapels. It was finished in 1230. It also has two cloisters, one Romanesque "las Claustrillas" (XII century) and a late gothic one, "San Fernando" (XIII and XIV centuries). Among the tombs are those of Alfonso VIII and his wife in the choir chapel, and that of Fernando de la Credo, son of Alfonso X.

The chapels of the Assumption and of El Salvador have mudejar elements. The San Fernando cloister has coloured plasterwork, as has the entrance to the sacristy. The chapter house contains the banner from the famous battle of Las Navas de Tolosa as well as collections of fabrics, garments and ornaments removed from royal tombs. These reveal a multitude of details related to weaving and costumes of the thirteenth century and onwards.
Hours: 10.30-2 and 4-6.30. Sundays: 10.30-3 only; slightly

shorter hours October to March. Closed all day Monday. 4 Euros entrance.

Hospital del Rey - a well-known resting place for tired or sick pilgrims. It is a large building, 12th to 16th c., with pilgrims' door, house and pharmacy and pilgrim imagery in the carvings. At the entrance is the Ermita de Santo Amaro, full of reminders of people cured of various diseases. The building has been recently restored and is now part of the law faculty of the University of Valladolid. It may be open on weekdays; information about opening times readily available. Opposite is the good-value Fonda Puerta Romeros.

On the eastern outskirts of Burgos, is the **Carthusian monastery,** the Cartuja de Miraflores, 4km from the centre and also sign-posted. This is an old Royal foundation, whose church was completed in 1498. Its sober facade belies the richness of the interior. Royal mausoleum in flamboyant Gothic style at the centre of the apse. Hours: 10.15-3 and 4-6. Sundays and holidays: 1-3 and 4-6. Open on Mondays.

Accommodation:
Refuge: Run by the ayuntanuento, beds, kitchen, evening meals are served. Open from May to October.

Cyclists and motorists interested in **El Cid can enjoy a 9km excursion** to the monastery of San Pedro de Cardena, on the Miraflores road. Opening times: 10-1.30 and 4-6; Sundays and holidays:12-1.30 and 4-6. San Pedro is a large, recently restored monastery which contains the family chapel of El Cid and the grave of his horse, Babieca. Restaurant opposite.

Time permitting, an optional detour to **Santo Domingo de Silos**, some 58km south of Burgos, is highly recommended. There is a bus service from Burgos (details available). The Abbey of Santo Domingo de Silos' cloister has the most inspired Romanesque sculpture in Spain. This includes scenes from the life of Christ, among them Jesus and the disciples on the road to Emmaus. Christ is dressed as a pilgrim. The small museum has an 11th c. mozarabic chalice of Santo Domingo. The Abbey is also famous for its Gregorian chant and recently issued a best-selling CD. Hours: 10-1 and 4.30-6, Sundays 4.30-6, open on Mondays. Guided tours only, last entry 6pm.7 Euros entrance.

Mass, with Gregorian chant, at 9am (Sundays 12 noon) and Vespers every day at 7pm.

Accommodation: In the monastery itself (men only, advance booking essential), Hostel Cruces (double 35 Euros), Hostel Arco San Juan across the river below the monastery, with peaceful garden (47 Euros double with bath). The Hotel Tres Coronas** is in the square not far from the monastery.

From Santo Domingo de Silos it is possible to avoid retracing one's steps back to Burgos by cutting across country to Castrojeriz via Lerma and Santa Maria del Campo. Lerma is a fortified, well-preserved town on a hill; castle of the Dukes of Lerma, several churches, also shops, banks, hotels, restaurants.

6km to Villabilla de Burgos
(837m) (1025)

Directions:
Church (left) on the other side of railway line. Cross minor/branch line but not the main (Madrid-Irun) line. Fork right, passing to the left of a house in front of a flour factory (right). Follow the road round to the right, cross a bridge over a river and turn left on other side, past 2 bridges on to a farm road through fields. (Main road ahead to left). Keep straight on for 1km till you reach the road. Turn left along it, cross to other side, and cross bridge over the river Arlanzon.

After bridge, fork left down a track parallel to main road and continue on it until it joins the road at entry to Tardajos.

4km to Tardalos
828m (1029)

This was the Roman town of "Augustobirga", and was situated on the Roman road. At the entrance to the town stands an eighteenth century iron cross. This marks the site of the former pilgrim hospital. In 1182 countess, Dona Mayor gave the hospital to the church of San Juan in Burgos. The donation was confirmed by Pope Lucious III : "In villa que dicitur Oterdaios ecclesiam S.Johannis cum hospitale.."

Accommodation:
Fonda/restaurant, Fernando is comfortable with double room

at 25 Euros. Bar next door may also have rooms. Rest Ruiz has good rooms and food. There is also a bakery and a grocery.
Refuge: Doctor's surgery in new building with sign 'Centro de Saludad'.
Directions:
Pass rollo on left on entry. Fork left opposite bar down Calle del Mediodia. Turn right at end and then left on to a minor road. Keep straight on to Rabe de las Calzadas.

1.5km Rabe de las Calzadas
(1031.5)
Fountain.
Directions:
Keep straight on through village and turn right in a triangular "square". Keep straight. Fork right at modern chapel (left) by cemetery (left) then fork left 50m further on.
Track joins from right and the path levels out to a vast, seemingly endless plateau.
This is the meseta, lush and green in spring, a dustbowl in summer. You will either find it extremely tedious or, if you like undulating expanses reaching out to infinity in all directions, hauntingly beautiful, especially in the early morning light. Although it is so far removed from the noise of "civilisation" it is, in fact, far from silent. The wind, the insects, the birds and the rustling grass can also be noisy in their own inimitable fashion.
500m further on path descends to a valley (approx. 1.5km to village ahead). Join UMUR coming from right. When you get to the road, cross it and enter village of Hornillos del Camino.

8.5km to Hornillos del Camino
(1040)
Small village with a large gothic church, formerly an important pilgrim halt with a hospital and a small Benedictine monastery.
The old rectory and pilgrim hospital stands at the entrance to the town. Alfonso VII gave this land to the monks of San Dionisio (St Denis) in Paris in 1156 to provide aid for the pilgrims. Later,

a Benedictine monastery was established, dependent on the French motherhouse of Rocamador. The foundation received gifts and privileges from Alfonso VIII, Fernando III, Fernando IV and Salfonso XI (1318). The church is representative of the grand epoch in which it was conceived and built. It is basically gothic, with a handsomely vaulted crossing and three aisles, all well preserved. A lovely statue of the Virgin of Rocamador
New refuge. Bar at end of village does basic meals. Fountain outside church.

Directions:
Continue to the end of the village (no shops or bars) and turn right at the public weighbridge. Turn left after 1km and fork right (i.e. keeping straight on) 500m further on. Fork right again after 10m, uphill all the time. Turn left at next junction.
At the top of the hill and beginning of the plateau cross a track and keep straight on.
Apart from electricity pylons in the distance to the left *there is no sign of any sort of habitation at all in any direction, giving a feeling of being on the "roof of the world".*
Keep straight on at next two junctions (first is a crossroad, second is a T junction. Turn left).
Cross a UMUR and keep straight on. Shortly afterwards track descends to valley. Keep right at fork. Cross another UMUR (ruined houses to left and right) and keep straight on uphill again. Turn left at next fork (i.e. straight on) and then the path levels out again. Nothing in sight for miles and miles around.
Cross a minor road and keep straight on (2 large clumps of trees away to right in distance). Cross grassy track and keep straight on. Cross another track and keep straight on again.
Two km past the last minor road a valley suddenly appears on your right. Keep straight on. 500m later another valley appears ahead and just after that another path joins from behind left. Then —all of a sudden- the church and village of Hontanas appears below you. Go down the path into the village, following the path to the right and then to the left down the main street. Fountain (left) and church (left).
Some 5km beyond Hornillos is the cool **'oasis' of Fuente Sambol,** 200 to 300 metres to the left of the Camino. Trees and

piped water to a trough. Very basic refuge here with straw to sleep on and water from the fountain. No w.c.

11km from Hornillos to **Hontanas**

(for cyclists approx. 40km from Burgos and worth the short detour)
A real pilgrim village (its name means "the fountains") dominated by its church (fountain beside it). No shop or hostel but 2 bars including one at the swimming pool, which normally opens in July and closes on 15 Sept. Nowhere to buy food in spring and autumn.

Accommodation:
Refuge (20) at the town hall is modern but no kitchen or shower. Also a private refuge which is not recommended for women travelling alone.
There are two bars. One near the swimming pool.

Directions:
Continue past fountain (left), church (left), weighbridge (right) and swimming pool (right). When you get to the road the way marks direct you to cross it and fork right (i.e. to left before you've crossed over) along a track on the other side. However, although this takes you off the road, parallel to it, there is hardly any shade at all and you may prefer instead, to stay on the road as it has very little traffic and is tree-lined almost all the way to Castrojeriz.

Otherwise, after crossing the road, turn left 300m further on, at a junction after three large trees. When you reach the ruins of the Molino del Cubo take the upper path (i.e. your height) and keep straight on, uphill slightly, to the ruin of San Miguel. Pass below it. The track then descends to join another from the right. Fork left. 10m later a track joins from behind left – keep straight on (still parallel to road). keep straight on at next fork. Track then veers left to join road. Follow it for 1km to the ruins of Hospital San Anton.

5km to **ruins of Hospital of San Anton**

(1056)
This monastery, founded by Alfonso VII in 1146, belonged to

the French order of the Antonines, suppressed in 1787 by a bull issued by Pope Pius VI. The existing fabric is fourteenth century and the greater part of it is gothic. The carretera passes under the arch; to the left is the great ruined door; to the right there survive two cupboard-like apertures where the monks and other charitable persons used to leave food for the pilgrims.

The Antonines had the reputation of being able to cure St Anthony's Fire, a disease that appeared in Europe in the tenth century. Sufferers were blessed with the Tau cross, and the protection of St Anthony implored on their behalf.

Directions:
Continue along tree-lined road (ruins of alcazar on hill above town visible ahead) to Castrojeriz.

3km **Castrojeriz**
(800m) (1059)
A Roman town, probably founded by Julius Caesar. It seems to be built in layers around the hill. Now visited only by pilgrims. The way in is long and it takes 20 minutes to walk from one end of the town to the other. Tourist Office near the Calle Cordon (may be open in summer only).
Shops, bars, restaurant, bank.
The churches of Santa Maria del Manano, Santo Domingo, Santiago de los Caballeros, San Esteban and San Juan are ample testimony to the past splendour of this town.
On the way into it you pass Santa Maria del Manzano, which dates from the ninth century. There are no visible remains of the original structure. The collegiate church that replaced it in 1214 was built by Dona Berenguela la Grande. It is transitional Romanesque, with five arches and later, mainly eighteenth century renovations. It is famous for the richness of its ornamentation. The main altarpiece is rococo (1767), with valuable paintings by Antonio Mengs, a German artist who was court painter to Carlos III. The polychrome stone statue of Santa Maria del Manzano is an exceptionally beautiful piece. In his "Cantigas", Alfonso X "el Sabio" related several miracles wrought by this Virgin, who is the subject of much local devotion.

Other interesting items are the statue of Santiago wearing a cloak adorned with scallop shells; the image of Nuestra Senora del Popolo, a fourteenth century Italian work; and another piece from Italy, La Piedad, by Bronzino. Outside, on either side of the main door stand two delightful sculptures: the Angel of the Annunciation and the Virgin.

A number of well known persons are buried in the church: the marquesses of Hinestrosa, counts of Rivadavia y Castro, Dona Leonora, queen of Aragon, and Alonso de Castro, who died at the battle of Zamora in 1476; abbots, and others. This great monument of the Way of St James was administered by a large number of canons, reduced to sixteen by the thirteenth century.

The church of Santo Domingo (XVI century) serves today as the parish church and guardian of valuable works of art from other churches. Its fine parish museum contains Flemish tapestries, a statue of Santiago Peregrino, another very lovely one of the Virgin dressed as a pilgrim, and a fine collection of vestments. The church of San Juan, gothic and recently restored, has a graceful nave and generous proportions. Its tower retains

Romanesque features; the cloister is fourteenth century.
Castrojeriz had numerous hospitals. The pilgrim Koenig, writing in 1495, mentioned four. At the beginning of the nineteenth century seven were still functioning : Nuestra Senora del Manzano, San Andreas, Santa Catalina, La Inmaculada Concepcion , San Juan, Nuestra Senora del Pilar, and San Lazaro.

Accommodation:
Hostel/Bar El Meson de Castrojeriz (T:947-37 74 00), Calle Cordon 1, is welcoming and helpful. Double room with all facilities 35 Euros, single 2300; good food with 1000 pta menu. They may be able to arrange for pilgrim record to be stamped and churches to be opened. Restaurant Anton (T:947-37 70 12), 50 yards away does rooms in house opposite the restaurant. Breakfast served late here. Hotel La Posanda tel: 947 37 86 10. Double 7300. Single 4200.
Refuge: (20) at the Albergue de Peregrinos, calle Cordon, at far end of town; turn right off main road. Bunk beds, kitchen and showers. Hot water in early months, but water may be turned off during summer from 8pm to 8am.
Campsite: Camping Camino de Santiago; leave the N120 at Villa-sandino. Open June 1 to September 30. There is also a class 2 campsite in Castrojeriz, between Santa Maria and Santo Domingo (with bar).
Directions:
Turn right at entrance to Castrojeriz to church of Nuestra Senora del Manzano and then turn left through village (very long). To leave, pass church of San Juan (right) and go down to road. Veer left to crossroads. Turn left, cross road and after 50m turn left down a UMUR. After 1.5km cross bridge over Rio Odrilla and shortly afterwards (house visible away to left), at staggered junction, keep straight on up path that winds its way, veering left, uphill to the top of the hill and the monument you can see on the skyline. You are back on the meseta again (1km from bridge). At the top keep straight on (i.e. don't turn left) towards iron crosses (way marks).
Keep straight on, following these way marks (crosses with yellow

plastic on them) and shortly afterwards, after approx. 500m you look down to a huge valley (bowl-like) below you. Panoramic views. From here the path leads more or less straight to Itero del Castillo (though it doesn't actually go into the village).

Descend on track through fields for 1-2km. Cross a farm road and keep straight on. Fork left slightly downhill when track divides. Cross another farm road and keep straight on and approx. 1km afterwards join a minor road, going slightly uphill, at the Fuente del Piojo (fountain).

Turn right along road for 1km to crossroads. (Itero de la Vega visible ahead). Turn left along road (ignore farm track back to left). Pass Ermita San Nicolas (left), which has now been converted into a refuge by the Italian association of the Friends of St James and then cross bridge over Rio Pisuerga – the boundary between the provinces of Burgos and Palencia. (The 65km stretch of the Camino which passes through Palencia is particularly rich in historic monuments.) Fork right on other side of bridge down minor road for 1.5km to village of Itero de la Vega.

10km to **Itero de la Vega**
(1069)

Small village. Thirteenth-century Ermita de la Piedad (with statue of St James the Pilgrim) at entrance to village, sixteenth-century church of San Pedro.

Key to the refuge (10) available from bar opposite. Bar found expensive. Shop.

Directions:

Keep straight on through village (Calle Coinde Vallellano, calle Santa Maria), cross end of main square (fountain, rollo). Continue straight on and then turn left down Calle Marques de Estrella, following white arrows painted on road. Turn right into Calle Comanante Ramirez. Pass five large trees (left, another fountain) and keep straight on to crossroads. Cross road and continue along UMUR flanked by water channels on either side. Pass turning (left) to hamlet of Bodegas after 1km and keep straight on. Cross bridge over Canal Pisuerga and continue straight on to top of hill (three humps visible ahead on skyline).

View of Boadilla del Camino (3km ahead) at the top.
Cross canal and turn right along bank. Then either follow street round to right to leave village or head for church to enter it.[RJ: fork right at fountain]

8km to **Boadilla del Camino**
782m(1077)

Its monumental fifteenth century jurisdictional marker ("rollo") is well known and is evidence of the importance once enjoyed by the village. Here criminals were exhibited, tied to an iron ring before being sent to the chief magistrate in Castrojeriz, to which town Boadilla owed allegiance.

The parish church is dedicated to Santa Maria and dates from the fifteenth and sixteenth centuries; it is mainly renaissance, with three aisles, and interlaced vaulting. Besides good paintings and sculptures there is an outstanding baptismal font, on small columns.

Refuge in same building at lower of two bars (key at bar); simple and friendly. Upper bar has shop.

Directions:
To leave continue past bar and then turn left alongside football ground (right) and left again past warehouse along UMUR. Keep straight on. Go through a gap in the irrigation channels (raised up) and 200m further on fork right up a bank to join the towpath of the Canal de Castilla. Keep straight on along it for 3km. Cross FB over the canal by a lock, veer right down a foot path down a bank, go along a tree-lined path for 100m and turn right onto road. Follow it, veering left under railway bridge to crossroads (by Tourist Office). [RJ: follow signs for "Astadillo" to bend in road (to right) and then cross canal at FB.]

6km to **Fromista**
(780m) (1083)

Small town with golden, Romanesque church of San Martin, one of the most perfect to be found on the route.

It was founded by queen Dona Mayor in 1035, and declared a National Monument when it was restored in 1893. The monastery, now disappeared, was administered by the Benedictines. The church is one of the most beautiful, perfect and complete examples of the Romanesque style, and has a deserved international reputation. The stone used in its construction is a light golden colour. It has three aisles, a crossing with lantern, and two cylindered towers. The decoration of its doors, their archivolts, the string-coarse, windows and capitals is exceptionally fine. Its proportions are perfect.

It contains a valuable life-size Romanesque crucifixion dating from the beginning of the thirteenth century, and a fifteenth century statue of Santiago Peregrino. The 315 exterior corbels, each one different, represent human and animal figures.

The Santa Maria del Castillo, which was erected on the site of the former castle or fortress, has been declared a National Monument. Gothic, with three naves and a renaissance doorway, its most notable feature is an altarpiece composed of 29 painted panels below gothic baldachins. The panels depict scenes from the life of Christ, and were executed by several different artists in a Spanish-Flemish style. (The panels are currently on loan in Palencia).

The church of San Pedro is also worth visiting. Its gothic fabric (XV century) incorporates vestiges of an earlier Romanesque church. It contains several paintings by the school of Ribera and two by Mengs. The main altarpiece is renaissance, and shows Italian influence. There are plans to convert the church into a museum of sacred art.

The hermitage of Otero de Santiago is a gothic structure with later renovations. It contains a polychrome statue of the Virgin, seated (XIII century).

Once there were several hospitals in this locality. The most important were those of Santiago, founded in 1507, San Martin, founded before 1453, and Los Palmeros, presently a hotel and restaurant near the church of San Pedro in the centre of the town. Nearby stands a monument to San Telmo, patron saint of navigators, who was born here.

Accommodation:
Can be difficult to find. The Fonda Marisa (no meals on Sunday) is recommended. The Pension Camino de Santiago (T:988-81

00 53) (28 Euros for a double), next to a playground, is also very good - ask for Mila. Just past the church of San Pedro and on left of main road is a posada with rooms at 18 Euros. Hotel San Martin, 50 Euros. menu is good at 1200. Pension Marisa c/San Martin 13, tel:979 81 00 23. Single 20 Euros. Hostal Telmo, double for 50 Euros. Centro de Turismo Rural tel: 979 81 10 28 is near Plaza San Telmo, Double 45 Euros. A good cheap restaurant is the Maga, calle Ingeniero Rivera, with a pilgrims' menu at around 75 Euros. Restaurant El Corte is good value and some bars may have crayfish tapas.

Refuge: Alberge de Peregrinos behind the Ayuntamiento, facing the main square. Try to arrive in good time as there is sometimes confusion over who books pilgrims in, the parish priest or the town hall.

Walkers only: 4km to Poblacion de Campos which has a small, new refuge in former school: 10 bunk beds, hot showers, garden and kitchen. Key from house with telephone sign. Shop opposite upper bar.

Directions:
To leave Fromista – keep straight on along road to Carrion de los Condes (i.e. cross road at crossroads by Tourist Office).
The new route now takes you alongside this road on a specially prepared senda de peregrino, running parallel to it like a cycle track all the way to Carrion de los Condes, passing the entrances to Poblacion de Campos and Villovieco, through Villarmentero de Campos and past the entrance to villalcazar de Sirga.
Or you can continue on the old route, turning right after 4km on the road into Poblacion de Campos.

4km to **Poblacion de Campos**
790m (1087)
Small village. 2 bars, shop (unmarked), very small refuge.
The parish church of La Magdalena is situated in the northerly part of the town. It is a good example of the baroque: spacious, with three aisles. In the centre of the altarpiece in the central niche stands a beautiful image of the penitent Magdalene.
The hermitage of el Socorro is in the centre of the town in the plaza del corro, and is transitional Romanesque in style. It

contains a thirteenth century polychrome statue of the Virgin, seated, for whom the hermitage is named.

The hermitage of San Miguel lies in the outskirts and is transitional Romanesque. The ancient hospitals ruins have been incorporated into a handsome modern house.

Accommodation:

Refuge (12) in a school. hot baths, kitchen. 5 Euros. Bar Las Ciguenas serves meals. Keys for refuge can be got from Senora Sastre.

Directions:

Fork right up concrete road (Paseo del Cementerio) to visit village, aiming for church. At junction behind church take minor road ahead with raised irrigation channel down left hand side. Otherwise, turn left past village, join above road and turn left. Keep straight on. After 3km pass a fountain on right hand side, built in 1989, with a wayside cross, shell and red/white cross motif. keep straight on to Villavieco.

3km to **Villavieco.**
(790m) (1090)

Directions:

Turn left over bridge over the river Ucieza and then immediately right along its bank and keep straight on. Follow the bank for 5km, as far as the Ermita de la Virgen del Rio (contains alabaster statue of St James the pilgrim).

Sometimes it is necessary to cross small irrigation channels running at right angles to the river – some have stepping stones- and then go back onto the path again. The last km is fairly shady.

Turn left along the road when you reach the ermita (a large building, similar to a church but now a private house) which is near a bridge. Then pass the Ermita del Cristode la Salud (small- still in use) (left) and after 1 km enter Villalcazar de Sirga.

6km to **Villalcazar de Sirga**
(809m) (1096)
Also known as "Villasirga".

The life of this historic town has revolved around the church of Santa Maria la Blanca, through the centuries. It was founded by the Templars in the thirteenth century and has the dimensions of a cathedral. Its plan is distinctive, with three naves, crossing and five apsidal chapels.

The great south doorway has 50 sculptures arranged in a double frieze. The Adoration of the Magi appears over the lower portion, and the Apostles, with Christ presiding, in the upper. The main altarpiece is decorated with painted panels, and belongs to the school of Pedro Berruguete.

The chapel of Santiago is a veritable museum of medieval sculpture. The most distinguished are the tombs of prince Felipe, the fifth son of Fernando "el Santo", and his second wife Dona Leonor Ruiz de Castro, together with that of an unknown knight. The tombs show funeral processions, with substantial traces of their original colouring. A large rose window, designed to admit the mid-day sun, lights the chapel.

The "Cantigas" of Alfonso X "el Sabio", together with the pilgrimage, have given the church its reputation:

Romeus que de Santiago	*Pilgrims to Santiago*
Ya forun-lle contando	*Were already being told*
Os miragres que a Virgen	*Of the miracles the Virgin*
Faz en Villa-Sirga	*Wrought in Villasirga*

The Virgen Blanca, seated and carved in stone, is set against a column near the chapel of Santiago. Another statue presides over the main altarpiece. The hermitage of the Virgen del rio contains a handsome alabaster statue of Santiago Peregrino. The town had two hospitals: the "Real", or "de las Tiendas", a hostelry which was obliged to provide pilgrims with basic shelter, and another which admitted lepers and other travellers.

Bar/shop. 2 mesons, fountain in public garden.

Accommodation:
None, apart from the refuge, the Albergue de Peregrinos (12), with kitchen, in the Plaza del Palacio. The Restaurante El Meson de Villasirga was until recently run by one of the great characters of the Camino, Don Pablo Payo and family. Small

shop. Bar south of church does good, simple food.
Directions:
Turn right to enter village. Otherwise keep straight on to main road. Turn right and continue along it, with cornfields to both sides in an undulating landscape.
This road is not usually busy but there is no shade at all. Bodegas in fields to side of road.

6km to **Carrion de los Condes**
(840m) (1102)
Busy town with good shops. All facilities.
Carrion was the capital of a territory ruled by the Beni Gomez family, rivals of El Cid, and of which his sons-in-law, the "infantes" or princes of Carrion were members. These noblemen, hoping to acquire the dowries belonging to El Cid's daughters, went to Valencia following the Comprador" conquest of the city. They wooed the girls with flattery and succeeded in marrying them. Returning northwards, they mistreated their brides and abandoned them on the road. El Cid's men at arms killed the "condes" in revenge. The girls later married the princes of Aragon and Navarre. The poem La Prise de Pampelune depicts Charlemagne passing through Carrion on his way to liberate the Way of St James from Arab domination.
The convent of Santa Clara (XIII century) was built by two of St Clare's companions. It preserves a good collection of artifacts and the church contains a sculpture of "La Piedad", by Gregorio Fernandez.
The name of Santa Maria del Camino church, or de la Victoria refers to the Camino de Santiago. It is Romanesque (XII century) and a National Monument, containing a collection of historically and artistically valuable objects. The entrance commemorates the tribute of the hundred maidens. Carrion was freed of this ignominious exaction thanks to the fracas created by a number of bulls at the spot where the maidens were to be handed over to the Moors. As a votive offering, a thanksgiving Mass was celebrated until very recently on the third day of Easter in the "capilla de la Victoria".
The church of Santiago was burned down during the War of

Independence in 1809. It retains its splendid Romanesque façade (XI century). The frieze is justifiably famous. The figure of Christ, beautifully carved, presides over the four Evangelists and the ranks of the Apostles. In the archivolts there appears the popular theme of musicians, each with a different instrument. The façade is a National Monument.

Nuestra Senora de Belen is on the outskirts to the north. The Virgin of this title is the patroness of the city. The gothic sanctuary contains a good plateresque altarpiece.

The monastery of San Zoilo is also a National Monument. It has always ministered generously to pilgrims. The fabric of the building has been much restored. Only vestiges of the Romanesque structure survive. The cloister is renaissance (1537), the work of Juan Badajoz, and was described by the writer and critic Camon Aznar as "one of the most wonderful renaissance cloisters in Spain." In it can be seen the tombs of the sons of the infamous counts of Carrion.

Accommodation:
Hostel Ia Corte, calle Santa Maria 34, across the road from the church, is good value (double for 40-45 Euros); room 103 has splendid view of church tympanum. Very good meals also (set menu 7 Euros). The Casa de Huespedes is run by the Restaurant El Resbalon (T:988-88 00 11), in a side street near Santa Maria. The rooms are near the restaurant which we will, in the light of our own experience be reluctant to recommend. The Convento de Santa Clara has a small guest wing with hot water and cooking facilities.

Hotel Real Monasterio San Zoilo tel: 979 88 00 49 is a luxary hotel with an expensive atmosphere. Restaurant Abel near the Santiago church has good food.

Refuge: Albergue de Peregrinos (30) adjoins the church of Santa Maria and is run by the priest. Welcoming, hot showers, garden but no kitchen.

Directions:
To enter town – turn left off road at flour factory. To leave – continue past square and church of Santa Maria and turn right. Pass in front of church of Santiago and veer left to cross

the river Carrion by the main bridge.

Pass in front of the Monastery of San Zoilo (left) and come to a large crossroads 300m later, keep straight on for 300m further, past a petrol station, to another crossroads where the N120 veers left. Keep straight on along a minor road which is signposted to "Villotilla6". Keep straight on for 4km.

Pass the Abadia de Benvivere (right), former abbey but now a private house, just before a sharp bend in the road where a bridge crosses a small river. 300m after the bridge there is a junction with a minor road: cross it and keep straight on along a farm road (scallop shell way mark) through cornfields. The landscape is flat in all directions, keep straight on for 2.5km to plantation of chopos (poplars). Cross it, keep straight on for 6km, ignoring turnings to left and right. The church tower and cemetery are visible to the right shortly before you enter the village of Calzadilla de la Cueva.

Cyclists, the exit from Carrion de los Condes is not easy to find. Head initially north (do not follow signs for Leon) until the N120 is met and then turn left in a westerly direction. The road, which seems to stretch in a straight line for miles, is level and wide with a good cycle track and picnic places at regular intervals.

IMPORTANT - At Carrion buy some food before leaving and make sure you have plenty of water. Between Carrion and the next main town of Sahagun is a long and arid plane with little accommodation (other than refuges) except for the hostel at Calzadilla de Ia Cueza, and only a few bars and shops.

Campsite: El Eden near river. tel: 979 88 01 85.

17km **Calzadilla de la Cueva**
(1119)
Bar/restaurant (has rooms). Shaded area with seats. At end of village (right).
Directions:
Continue straight on through village to road. Cross the river Cueza and keep straight on the road, passing the remains of the eleventh century pilgrim hospital, formerly very important, of Santa Maria de las Tiendas.

2km to **Ledigos**
883m (1125)
Directions:
At entrance to village fork left off road and continue on track through fields parallel to road, emerging to rejoin it after bend at exit, crossing the river Cueza again. keep straight on road.

4km to **Terradillos de los Templarios** (1129)
Shop, fonda. Eighteenth-century church of San Pedro.
Directions:
Continue on the main road, passing turnings to the left to Morationos and then San Nicolas del real Camino(fountain).
After this you leave the province of Palencia to enter Leon. There is a fair amount of traffic on this stretch (but less on Sundays , when there are no heavy goods vehicles) and the stretch from Calzadilla de la Cueza to Sahagun can therefore be rather tedious. Sahagun is now visible ahead.
After this you can either (a) continue along the road for 7km more, directly to Sahagun, turning off the N120 at the flour mill or (b) turn right off the road, shortly after the provincial boundary, onto a track. Turn left along a clear track which now runs parallel to main road, keep straight on through fields, ignoring turnings to left and right. Panoramic views. Then, at large rubbish tip (probably smoking) another track joins from the right. Here you can either turn left and return to the road again at KM235 (and in which case you will simply have done a "rodeo" to get away from the traffic for a while, admire the view and perhaps have a quiet sit down) or keep straight on downhill, aiming for the river Valderaduey at the bottom, opposite the Ermita Virgen del Puente on the other side (a former pilgrim hospice). This is the old route. There is no longer the bridge at this point but as the river is extremely shallow (only a few inches deep) it should normally be possible to cross it.
(If you rejoined the road again after the rubbish tip, keep straight on road until after you have crossed the road bridge over the Valderaduey. Turn right immediately along a track along

the river bank for 100m until you reach the ermita. Trees and a good place for a rest.)
The path leading from here into Sahagun is still known as the Camino frances de la virgen. Turn left at the ermita and follow the path until you reach the embankment on the Sahagun bypass. Turn left under bridge and keep straight on other side, aiming for a very large white grain silo ahead. When you get there, cross N120 and enter Sahagun.

11km to **Sahagun**
(816m) (1140)

Cluny, which had a not inconsequential influence on the Camino de Santiago established its most important institution for pilgrims here. Sahagun once had five hospitals, but only the monastery of San Facundo could provide 60 beds in the eleventh century and was collecting 2000 measures of wheat in the fifteenth. The monastery, now a ruin, was the former owner of museum pieces to be found in collections all over Europe and America. The monastery had jurisdiction over 90 other religious houses and had privileges similar to those of Cluny.

Sahagun is the centre from which the best mudejar style spread throughout the region. The thirteenth century church of San Lorenzo is outstanding, the best of the religious buildings in this area. It has three apses with a frieze of blind arches on the exterior walls, profuse exterior decoration and a tower over the lady chapel. The church of San Tirso, also displaying the "brick Romanesque" style of the twelfth century, was one of the first churches built by morisco workmen. It has three aisles, crossing and a chancel with a trapezoidal chapel, a drum shaped apse and a tower above the lady chapel. Like San Lorenzo it contains a wooden mudejar ceiling (XV century).

In the southern outskirts stands the former Franciscan monastery of La Peregrina (XIII century), also mudejar in style, with later modifications. The image of the Virgin, with the accoutrements of a pilgrim, is in San Lorenzo.

The churches of La Trinidad and San Juan de Sahagun are equally distinguished. The last is baroque and contains a beautiful gothic sculpture of the city's patron, San Facundo, the work of Gregorio Fernandez.

On one side of San Tirso and the ruins of the Cluniac abbey stands the Benedictine convent (las Madres Benedictinas). This is a modest building which contains a fascinating museum of Sacred Art particularly metalwork and sculpture.

The monastery ruins, San Tirso, San Lorenzo and La Peregrina, and the Romanesque monastery of San Pedro de las Duenas, off the Camino five kilometres to the south, have been declared National Monuments.

Accommodation:
Hostel Conde is recommended for its rooms and food , the Hostel Alfonso VI is new and comfortable (double with bath 35 Euros), and the Hostel La Codorniz, calle Arco s.n. (i.e. no number) at the top of the town near the station is also reasonably priced with good food. They take groups in July but do check. Fonda La Bilbaina/Mes6n Aranzazu at Avda Jose is another alternative. Antonio 121, near the station, has an English-speaking host. Double without bath 22 Euros. The La Asturiana, Calle Lesmes Franco 2, is good value with rooms at 2000 (double). They do not serve food. In contrast, the guest house run by the Madres Benedictinas charges around 38 Euros for a double room. They

are generally full in July and August. Good meals at the Bar/Restaurant Pacho and Bar/Restaurant Luis, Plaza Mayor 4.

Refuge: This has to be updated, information is unavailable.

Campsite: Pedro Ponce, class II site, open 15 April to 30 Sept., by River Cea and sports complex. Swimming pools free to campers but caps ('gorro') compulsory. Restaurant is basic. Crowded in summer.

Cycle Repairs: Garaje Redondo, calle Ia Vega 14 (2nd left past the arch).

Directions:

After crossing the main road continue down a small street (Calle Rounda Estacion). As you approach the railway line (the station is on your left) follow it for a short distance and cross at the bridge. Keep straight on down the Calle Jose Antonio, the Calle del Peso (fork right after this for the town centre), the Calle Rua and the Calle de las Monjas. You will soon run into an open space. The Convent of the Madres Benedictinas and the museum of religious painting is on your right. (Turn right here for the Arco de San Benito and the church of San Tirso).

To leave Sahagun continue straight from the Calle de las Monjas along the Calle de Rey Don Antonio and out of the town across the bridge over the river Cea.

This is bordered by poplar trees. Folklore has it that at a time when the Moors and Christians were battling for control of northern Spain, a Christian force camped near Sahagun. Before going to bed, some of the men stuck their lances in the ground. They woke the next morning to find that their weapons had sprouted roots, branches and leaves!.

Pass the swimming pool (right) and follow the main road To Leon to Calzada del Coto.

Between Sahagun and the next town, Mansilla de las Mulas, cyclists can follow the southern camino alternative, the Real Camino Frances (see below) and thus avoid the main road. Take the N120 out of Sahagun and watch out for yellow arrows. Modern Camino signs enable you to stick to the main road.

5km to **Calzada del Coto** - has shop, bar and refuge. (1146)

Leave the road here along a turning to the right.
At this point the camino divides, the two paths running more or less parallel to each other with the railway line in between them for much of the way. They merge at Mansilla de las Mulas.

A. CALZADA DE LOS PEREGRINOS

This is an old Roman road, the Via Trajana. Isolated. Little or no water. No accommodation worth speaking about. No shops or bars and virtually no shade from the sun for 30km. Emphatically not recommended in July or August. However, energetic walkers who enjoy space, silence and solitude will find this route to their satisfaction. You are advised to carry a good supply of food and water and embark on your voyage of greater adventure before the crack of dawn. There are precious few way marks. Not difficult to follow as there are few turnings. You are always going in a straight line due west. This applies to the rest of the Camino too.

Directions:

Turn right into the village of Calzada del Coto past the Ermita de San Roque on your right and follow the street through the village. At the end ignore the track to the left (this leads to Bercianos) and keep straight on (right). After 2km cross the bridge over the railway line (artificial lake to left on other side) and keep straight on.

You enter a wooded area, going gradually uphill. Small sparse trees and a little shade. After 3 km (from the railway bridge), just before you leave the woods, pass the Granja Valdelocajos, a large farm with modern houses and some large dogs. Be warned, they are not on leash! 1 km further on your right, is the new Fuente de los Peregrinos and a picnic area. Keep straight on for 3km and you reach Calzadilla de los Hermanos.

9km **Calzadilla de los Hermanos**
Directions:
Get to the village and keep straight on the main street, past the ermita (left) and continue to the end where a road joins from

behind right.

Continue. You cross an immense plateau stretching to the horizon on all sides. You can occasionally see the poles along the railway line away to the left and the grain silo at El Burgo Ranero. You may hear a train in the distance. All around you are cornfields stretching out to infinity.

After 3.5km you reach a junction where the camino is no longer tarred. It continues as a UMUR, on the other side of the tarred road intersecting it (left to El Burgo Ranero, right to Villamartin de D. Sancho). Keep straight on for 13.5km, ignoring any turnings left and right, until you reach the deserted railway station. Please note that apeadero means "halt, stopping place"). Hence Apeadero Villamarco.

17km **Apeadero Villamarco**

Trains stop here on request.

Directions:

Do not cross the railway line at the station (the road on the other side leads to the village of Villamarco, some 2km to the south). Keep straight on more or less parallel to it. After 4 km you pass through the valleys of two dried up rivers. There are occasional tracks to left and right. Keep straight on. After a further 6km you will enter two more valleys. The path veers left. Stick to it. There is a junction 200m after you emerge from the second valley. Keep straight on and the church tower of Reliegos appears suddenly. If you want to get there (bar) and end by the Camino Real Frances don't deviate. Your target is about 500m away, Alternatively, turn right down a track soon after the junction. Go downhill along a track in a straight line for 6km until you reach Mansilla de las Mulas. Alert travellers will have already caught a glimpse of it in the distance as they approach Reliegos. Enter the town by a canal. Turn left along the main road. Proceed straight to junction. You are in the town. Stick to the main street.

B. CAMINO REAL FRANCES

This route passes to the south of the other one. It leads directly west. Much of it now resembles a cycle track, consciously prepared for the "invasion" in the 1993 Holy Year. It is tree-lined on one side with picnic spots.

When you turn off the main road from Sahagun towards Calzado del coto, do not enter the village but take the left turn along an UMUR lined with trees.

This is the road to Bercianos. Despite its not being tarred, many vehicles use it, sending up irritating clouds of dust in the dry summer months.

Pass a laguna (right) after 1.7km. After 2km, you get to the Ermita de Perales (left). Go straight. After 1km cross the bridge over the river Coso (probably dry). You are now in the village of Bercianos del Real Camino.

5km to **Bercianos del Real Camino**
(1151)

There's an appealing renaissance sculpture of John the Baptist and a painting of the Calvary (both XVI century) in the church of El Salvador. In 1186 Fernando II of Leon gave the church of Santa Maria in Bercianos to the hospital at O Cebreiro.

Accommodation:
Very basic refuge in big, old parish house; key at first house on right (with back to refuge). Best avoided if possible. In 1953 it was reported to have a not ingnificant mice presence. Two shops. Rooms and meals at Hostal-Restaurante Rivero. Tel: 787 78 42 87.

Directions:
Follow the main road through the village. About 7km away, you will see the silos of El Burgo Ranero.

It was between these two places that the seventeenth-century Italian pilgrim, Domenico Laffi, was startled by the body of a fellow pilgrim who had been devoured by wolves. This was, and still is, one of the loneliest stretches of the entire pilgrimage.

Continue west along the intelligently defined track until you reach the village of El Burgo Ranero.

7km to **EL Burgo Ranero**

(1158)
Shop, bar/restaurant, fonda, refuge.

Accommodation:
Fonda Lozano has very good rooms and food. Affable proprietor. Breakfasts and lunches prepared. Renowned for its coffee. Also Bar/restaurant El Peregrino opposite the Albergue. If you care about such things watch prices carefully. Small shop near church. Refuge (30) at the Albergue de Peregrinos, a new, brown adobe house between the Plaza Mayor and large sports court. Thirty bunk beds in 4 rooms, kitchen, hot showers and lockable lockers.

Directions:
Follow the main road through the village past the church (right), cross a road that intersects the village from north to south and pass the cemetery (left).
2km further on the left is a group of ten trees (which you will see in advance) with a brick fountain set back from the road – a good place for a rest.
Keep straight on. The road carries straight on, and after 6km

passes a turning on the left, to the village of Villamarco (the village itself is 1km off route).
2km further on, the route crosses the railway line and continues with this on the left for a while. The route is clearly way marked with yellow arrows. It leads you to a small valley, crossing first the "river" Valdearcos. 1km on, it takes you over the Santa Maria River usually dry.
Shortly after this there is another shaded area with trees and the landscape becomes less flat, with bodegas (storage cellars for keeping wine cool) set into the hilly ground at intervals. 2km later you are in Reliegos.

13.5km to **Reliegos**
(1171.5)
Accommodation:
Has a good refuge (50+) with bunk beds and hot shower. Key from Bar Avoces, on left on way out of village. 'Sello' and good bocadillos there. Bar Gil, 10 Euros menu. Spar shop down the road.
Directions:
Keep straight on through village and exit the other side on a stony track across a plain, where you will get an outline of Mansilla de la Mulas 6km away. Continue west until you reach the main road. Cross it and the bridge over the canal and you are in the town.

6.5km to **Mansilia de las Mulas**
(799m) (1178)
We do not know when the town of Mansilla was founded, but it can barely have been before 1181, the date when Fernando II of Leon gave it a charter and made it a dependency of Benavente.
It was a fief of the count of Benavente until 1594, when the castle was destroyed. The town still retains some sections of its walled enclosure, with battlements and defensive towers.
Today there remain two churches open for worship: the ancient parish church of Santa Maria, and the chapel of Nuestra

Senora De Gracia, on the carretera from Valladolid. There are other churches which are disused; San Martin (XIV century) has been converted into a library. Of the monastery of San Agustin, only its ruins remain. The sites of San Nicolas, San Lorenzo and the monastery of San Adrain survive, the latter outside the walls to the east.

There were once three pilgrims hospitals. The parish church posesses the Rule of the Hospital of Sancti Spirytus and Santiago, dated 1570.

A little past km.309 on the right, lies the road that leads to the monastery of San Miguel de Escalada, 12km.away. It is the richest and best example of mozarabic architecture in Leon and was declared a National Monument in 1886. It has apses with round-headed Moorish arches, and arcades with marble columns that show Visigoth influence; some of the capitals show asturian influence as well. The church was consecrated in 913.

Santa Maria de Sandoval, 4km.off the carretera to the left is Cistercian Romanesque (XII century) and a National Monument. From the carretera, at km 311, an unpaved road on the right leads to the hill of Lancia. This was the seat of the most important city of the Astures, conquered by Romans in 19 B.C.

Shops, bars, restaurant, hostel, campsite.

Accommodation:

Accommodation may be difficult and best avoided, apart from the refuge. Fonda Las Faroles is adequate (28 Euros for double room) but the Bar Delicias should be avoided unless you are stuck. Also Bar Alonzo in square. Restaurant on square just before the bridge going out of the town, with white tiles round the door, is welcoming and has good food.

Refuge (30) in the Casa del Peregrino, calle del Puente, is excellent, with beds, hot showers and kitchen with pans. If closed ask in the square for the caretaker, Senor Pedrin, who has the key; he may be in the Bar Bodeguilla. Older and separate part of the refuge has no cooking facilities and is used for the overflow in summer.

Cycle Repairs: two shops, both on the main N601, one at each end of the town.

Directions:
Continue along the main street to the end of the town. Cross the bridge over the river Esla. Fork left onto the old road and then onto a track which largely continues parallel to the main road for 5km until you reach the village of Puente Villarente.
Detour for cyclists: a 15 km recommended detour, just out of Mansilla, to the right, past km 309, is to San Miguel de Escalada. A guide is there in summer months but generally not on Sundays. Light is best in the afternoon. No accommodation here. A pleasant extension is to continue past the church and return to the N601 at Villasabarrieg via Mellanzos.

6km to **Puente Villarente**
(1184)
Small village with fine bridge of 20 arches.
Accommodation:
Hostel Montane, with double rooms at 30 Euros and a 1000 pta menu, is useful and right by the camino. Also Bar La Maitana before walkers turn right off the road. Another hostel just over the bridge on the west side of river and north side of road is not

recommended unless you are stuck. Bar Avenalleda provides meals.

Directions:

The Camino follows the main traffic laden road to Leon. As you leave Puente Villa ante, there's a petrol station to the right. There's a way marked path to the right but is not easy to follow. In theory, it should go as far as Valdafuente (bar, farmacio) before rejoining the road again.

As you near Leon, fork left. Road veers right at Avenida de Madrid. Cross the river Torio at Puente Castro (by the FB). Advance to roundabout with fountains gurgling merrily among some engaging modern sculptures. Cross road and veer right along Calle Santa Ana (behind church with the same name) into the centre of Leon and the cathedral via the Calle Barahona, Calle Puertamoneda. Pass the church of Santa Maria del Mercado (right), and the Calle de la Rua.

Cyclists please note that the road to Leon becomes very busy, sometimes menacingly so, and the cycle track disappears. Both sides of the road are dominated by bleak concrete buildings dedicated to industry. The sooner you take leave of this grim landscape, the better for your aesthetic health. The road climbs steadily as it nears Leon but the gradient is never intimidating. Do not turn off the main road, cycle directly towards the centre of Leon.

13km to **Leon**

(822m) (1197)

Aymeric Picaud claimed that Leon was one of the largest cities in Spain, "royal and ecclesiastical", " full of every kind of enjoyable thing".. It is of Roman origin and grew out of the camp established by the Seventh Legion.

It had an enclosure with four gates, whose walls are well restored and survive in almost their entirety. With the Arab invasions Ordono II turned Leon into the capital of the Christian kingdom (910-924), and under Alfonso VII (1135) it continued to be an imperial city, with fiefdoms all over Spain and more beyond the Pyrenees. In the thirteenth century it was incorporated into the kingdom of Castile, and lost its dominance.

In the twelfth century the church of Santa Ana was a dependency of the church of the Holy Sepulchre in Jerusalem. In the same century it passed to the Order of St John of Jerusalem, whose cross appears over the west door. Nearby stood the leper hospital of San Lazaro, the hospital of Santo Sepolcro and the French quarter.

Santa Maria del Mercado was once called Santa Maria del Camino; though it is Romanesque, its existing structure dates from no earlier than the twelfth century, and it retains vestiges of several architectural styles. Behind it lies the plaza del Grano with its monumental neoclassical fountain decorated with two naked cherubs, symbols of the two rivers that embrace the city. Below the plaza's arcades, leathers are tanned for saddlers and shoemakers. Until the construction of the plaza Major nearby, markets were held here, and sellers of grain had their stalls. A restored stone cross marks the spot where sentences and judgments were made public. At the far end stands the Benedictine convent of Santa Maria de Carbajal.

The monastery of la Concepcion, on the left, was founded in 1518, making use of an old manor house belonging to the Quinones family (XIV century). Although it contains relicts and paintings of merit, the building's chief ornament is its external decoration.

Several important buildings are located in the plaza de San Marcelo. The church of San Marcelo contains the relics of the city's patron in a silver reliquary, and a crucifix attributed to Gregorio Fernandez. Only the tympanum of the door, and the lower part of the tower, remain of the former building, which was remodelled extensively, most recently in 1627.

The Ayuntamiento (XVII century) is by Vale Zanetti and has splendid stained glass windows. Gaudi's Casa de Botines bears the inimitable stamp of the great Catalan artist. At right angles to it is the noblest and handsomest of all Leon's palaces, the Palacio de los Guzmanes (XVI century), now the Diputacion Provincial. The interior has a large patio with two galleries supported on columns, windows provided with well-wrought grilles and balconies with sturdy balustrades. Near San Marcelo once stood the pilgrim hospital of San Antonio Abad. Facing the Diputacion is the chapel dedicated to Santo Cristo de la

Victoria, built, according to tradition, on the site of the house of San Marcelo, a Roman centurion of the Seventh Legion and a Christian martyr.

The cathedral, the "pulchra Leonina" is the most beautiful of Spain's gothic cathedrals. It was begun in 1205 and its main structure was already complete twenty years later. It occupies the site of some Roman baths an an ancient Romanesque church. The cathedral was modelled on Rheims and Amiens, and is built in the form of a Latin cross, with three aisles, and richly sculptured doorways opening on the aisles and the transepts. The west front is impressive, flanked by two towers, the bell-tower to the north (64.6 metres metres high) and the clock-tower to the south (67.8 metres high). In the column dividing the west door stands Nuestra Senora la Blanca and on her right an effigy of Santiago Peregrino on a column worn by the hands of pilgrims and scarred by contact with medallions and rosaries.

There are other images related to the pilgrimage in the cathedral. Beside the north door is a painting of San Cristobal (St Christopher), patron saint of travellers and pilgrims. The altarpiece of the high altar contains panels showing the translation of the body of St James in a cart pulled by two wild bulls, and a pilgrim approaching the saint's tomb. The sepulchre of bishop Martin Rodriguez in the north transept shows a relief representing the distribution of alms to pilgrims. The cathedral's doorways are justly celebrated for their sculptural ornamentation. Its most memorable feature, however, is its stained glass:125 windows, 57 roundels and three enormous rose windows, which together comprise a total of 1800 square metres of glass. The windows date from every century between the thirteenth and the twentieth, and relate stories of the lives of Christ, the Virgin and the Saints in an uninterrupted sequence, with a great variety of decorative motifs. The beauty of the glass in the capilla mayor is outstanding, as it that of the crossing. The walls of this cathedral account for an incredibly small area of the total interior surface; the stone can only complement the glass.

The trascor has alabaster and gilded figures dating from the renaissance (XVI century). The choir is one of the oldest in

Spain and reflects Flemish influence. The plateresque screen of the capilla mayor, the altarpiece and the silver urn that contains the relics of San Froilan (the work of Enrique de Arfe, XVI century), are all worth seeing. The cloister combines gothic and renaissance elements. From it you can enter the Diocesan Museum, one of the best of its type, with more than 1500 works from various schools and styles, many of inestimable value.

The Real Basilica de San Isidoro is one of the few churches that Aymeric Picaud ordered pilgrims to visit: In the city of Leon, it is essential to visit the venerable body of San Isidoro, bishop and confessor or doctor who established a most pious rule for the clerics of his church, instilling his teachings into the Spanish population and honouring the Holy Church with his excellent writings. The basilica is considered one of the jewels of early Romanesque art. It was built on the western corner of the Roman camp, possibly on the site of a temple of Mercury later occupied by a church dedicated to San Juan that was probably very similar to that of San Salvador in Valdedios. In 966 another was built in honour of the child martyr San Pelayo. Both were demolished at the end of the tenth century by Almanzor.

In the eleventh century, the remains of San Isidoro were transferred to this spot by Fernando I and his wife Dona

Sancha. Perhaps because the old church was felt to have little value (it may have been rebuilt in brick and adobe after its destruction by the Moors), another was built on a new ground plan and dedicated to San Isidoro (1063) and was one of the first Romanesque churches on the pilgrimage road. Dona Urraca effected and later enlarged the church (1073-1100).

The Pantheon Real which survives from this area is the burial place of eleven kings, twelve queens, twenty-three princes and various members of the nobility. It was a rectangular space, divided into three aisles with an intersecting barrel arch and pilasters with supporting columns; the freestanding ones are of enormous girth in relation to their height. The capitals derive their motifs from classical depictions of vegetation, but are disproportionate and rather coarsely executed. The very early Romanesque and its more developed version meet in this space. The paintings that cover the ceiling and walls almost all date from the twelfth century. The capitals are the churches' oldest sculptures, somewhat rude but possessing an expressive and extraordinary vigour. The Christ Pantocrator, seated above a rainbow and surrounded by the Evangelists, presides over the central arch. The magnificence of this crypt has led to its being given the title of the Sistine Chapel of Romanesque art.

The collegiate church is considered the most complete expression of the Romanesque style, lacking nothing: architecture, capitals and historic tympana, paintings, metalwork, ivories, illuminated manuscripts, documents on parchment etc. Visits can be made to its museums —with collections drawn from a wide variety of styles, beginning with Roman inscriptions – the treasury, the library, and the cloister. At the same time the famous agate chalice (XI century), the casket comprised of eleventh century ivories, the banner of San Isidoro embroidered with the hand of Santiago (1174), the tenth century Visigoth Bible, etc. are also on display.

The basilica has two doorways of great stylistic importance, typical of "pilgrimage Romanesque"; the Cordero (Lamb) doorway, with the scene of the sacrifice of Isaac and the mystic Lamb; and the Perdon, with the Descent from the Cross, the work of Master Esteban who also sculptured the Puerta de las

Platerias in Santiago de Compostela.

The Hospital of San Marcos. From the point where the calle Suero de Quinones opens onto the plaza de San Marcos, a modest two-storey building can be seen on the right. This was the pilgrim hospital. Next to it stands the renaissance building that was the Mother House of the Order of the Knights of Santiago of the Sword (1170).

In the twelfth century, near the bridge that crossed the river Bernesga, Dona Sancha built a hospederia for the "pauperes Christi". In the same century the friars who had converted themselves into a military order arrived. At the beginning of the sixteenth century the building was in poor condition, prompting the reconstruction begun in 1513 and lasting until well into the eighteenth century. The result was a beautiful example of Spanish renaissance architecture, in its most dignified and harmonious form. Medallions, shells, columns and pilasters ornament the façade. On the east side stands the gothic church, unfinished, with its entrance protected by a vast rounded arch. In the centre, the main entrance divides the whole edifice in two, according to the date of construction: the east wing is sixteenth century, and the west, close to the river, eighteenth. The frieze contains representations of soldiers, mythological figures and later Masters of the Order of Santiago.

Inside, the notable features are the cloister, the sacristy, the staircase, which gives access to the chapter house (in large part the work of Juan de Badajoz, "el Mago", who built the magnificent cloister of San Zoilo in Carrion de los Condes) and the choir where among others Juan de Juani and Guillen Doncel worked.

Today San Marcos is a lavish modern hotel which, at the same time, houses the Provincial Archaeological Museum, with an excellent collection of Roman inscriptions and coins, as well as valuable pieces of medieval and later sculpture and metalwork. The Hospital of San Marcos was the best known and most celebrated of the Order's hospitals connected with the pilgrimage, although there were many more – documents from seventeen others survive.

Other monuments of interest in Leon are the church of San

Martin (XI century, restored in the XVIIIth), that of El Salvador, with the remains of a Romanesque chapel, the Palace of the marquesses of Villasinda (XVI century), and that of the Counts of Luna, in a lamentable condition but with a handsome gothic doorway and portions built in a variety of other styles.

Accommodation:
Hostel Residencia Reina (T:987-20 52 12), calle Puerta la Reina Hostel Don Suero, av. Suero de Quinones 15, between San Isidoro and San Marcos, is noisy but convenient. Hostel El Bayon (T:987-23 14 46), calle Alcazar de Toledo 6; Hotel Paris(T:987-23 86 00), calle del Generalissimo Franco (main street, convenient for Cathedral, double room around 40 Euros,) Fonda Orvieto (T:987-22 22 36), av. de Roma, has bike storage (double room 25 Euros), Hospedaje Suarez, calle Generalissimo Franco7-2 is cheap (20 Euros double) and central. The Pension Americana (T:987-25 16 54) in the Avenida Ordono II (continuation of Gen. Franco) is simple and old-fashioned. Sign visible near turning to Calle Cap. Cortes; 14 Euros single. The Guzman el Bueno (T:987-23 64 12), Lopez Castrilldon 6 is a little more expensive (45 Euros for a double) but recommended. Youth Hostel at Infanta Dona Sancha Corre-dera 4 (YHA card needed) is open in July and August and has swimming pool, but may not be useable. Leon has plenty of restaurants: try the Plaza de San Martin area (Rest. Nuevo Racimo de Oro) and narrow roads off calle Generalissimo Franco. Cafeteria/Rest. Catedral, calle Meruana D. Berrueta (side street near Cathedral) has a 7 Euros menu. Also Bar La Cepadana in same street has 6 Euros menu. Bar Zalacain c/ La Rua 24 has vegetarian food.

Hostal Oviedo, Avda de Roma 26 tel: 987 22 22 36. near train station, bikes are accepted. Pension Sandoval, Plaza San Francisco 19, tel: 987 21 20 41. rooms 30 Euros. Hotel Paris c/Ancha 20. tel: 987 23 86 00. Double room 100 Euros.

Refuge: refuge accommodation is never easy in Leon. In 1993 a college, well away from the centre was used, and in 1992 San Isidoro provided a small and basic refuge (entrance in Plaza de San Martino round the back of the monastery). The Albergue de Leon (112) Collegio de Huerfanos Ferrovias. Avenida del Parque near the river in La Castra has all modern facilities.

Cycle Repairs: Bicicletas Blanco, calle Teniente Andres Gonzalez 1, Barrio Santa Ana, tel.(987) 20.96.10. Bicicletas Carlos, avda Facultad 29, tel.(987) 25.42.09. Also one in av. Suero de Quinones, between San Isidoro and San Marcos.

Directions:

To exit Leon, cross bridge over Rio Bernesga by the Hotel San Marcos. Go straight past public garden (Parque Quevedo, right, recommended for rest/picnic; black swans serenely gliding through the placid waters of the lake add to your enjoyment) and continue along this road. Turn left fork. Cross the railway line by FB. Go straight, passing the Iglesia Capilla de Santiago (right). Keep straight on uphill all the time. Turn right at a bus stop and some traffic lights halfway on hill into the Camino de la Cruz, which veers round to the left (still uphill) between bodegas. Continue. At junction 300m later another track emerges from left. Keep straight on (left) on UMUR (not road) by scrap dealers.(This may appear tricky but all you are doing is indulging in a game of "hide and seek" to avoid the busy main road.)

Keep straight on, passing factories. Forking right uphill (away from main road) at marble factory. At top of hill continue on track from left (the very tall spire of the modern church of Virgen del Camino is visible) and fork left by long wall on right.

At start of residential area (Calle Tras las Casas) fork (not turn) left onto tarred road ahead (leading towards church spire). Continue down Calle del Orbigo and take second left into the Calle Cervantes. Turn right onto main road, continuing to church in Virgen del Camino.

6km to **Virgen del Camino**
(905m) (1203)

What is today the village and sanctuary of La Virgen del Camino was – at the beginning of the sixteenth century – no more than a tiny hermitage on a bare hilltop traversed by the Camino Frances.

Between 1502 and 1511 a shepherd called Alvar Simon experienced visions of the Virgin, asking him to build her a shrine on the site of the existing hermitage.

The church became a place of pilgrimage, due to the many miracles worked by the image placed there, and the Virgin became the patroness of this part of Leon. The major feasts are celebrated on 15 and 29 September, and on 15 October.

The existing sanctuary was inaugurated in 1961. It is bold and modern in design, the work of Portugese Dominican architect Coello. In the façade stand thirteen colossal bronze sculptures six metres high, by the Catalan artist Subirachs. The four bronze doors are by the same artist. The first on the south side, which opens on the niche where the image of the Virgin stands, depicts the miracle of her appearance. Inside is preserved the baroque altarpiece of 1730, and in the centre of it, on a silver throne, "La Piedad", a sixteenth century work.

Since 1954 the sanctuary has been cared for by the Dominican Fathers, who also administer the "Fundacion de la Virgen del Camino", a large complex providing religious, cultural and social amenities. The rest of the complex is directly opposite the sanctuary on the other side of carretera.

Accommodation:
Hostal Julio Cesar tel: 987 30 01 29 Rooms 30 Euros. Hostal Sato, tel: 987 80 29 25. Rooms 35 Euros. Hostal Central tel: 987 30 20 41. Rooms 35 Euros. Bar El Peregrino serves food.

Directions:
Cross the road after (visiting) the church. Continue on minor road downhill behind crash barrier (to left) (signposted "Fresno del Camino 3.5km") leading to cemetery.
100m later the two caminos divide, to Hospital de Orbigo, some 25km, depending on your choice. You have two options:
a) traditional (road) route and
b) a recently way marked, longer alternative which passes to the south of N120 on minor roads.

A. Road option via VILLADANGOS DEL PARAMO :

Continue up hill past cemetery (left). Rejoin road in front of a factory. Continue on path above road (left). Ahead of you is a complicated motorway junction.
When you rejoin the road cross the first part (a slip road) carefully at yellow arrows painted on the road. Walk on the hard shoulder of the main Madrid-Astorga road. Keep straight. Go under both bridges and continue straight along the road.

Accommodation: Hostal Libertad. Menu at Restaurante Pradela. Refuge (36) Minicipal kitchen, hot water showers, bunks and bike storage. Key from Senora Rosario Franco who lives behind refuge.

4km **Valverde de la Virgen**
(887m) (1207)
Bar, fuente.

2km **San Miguel del Camino**
(1209/286)

Directions:
Shortly after San Miguel fork left off road onto parallel track. Veer right at farm and follow track across open land more or less parallel to road. When your instinct tells you that you are

going to rejoin the road ignore it. Instead keep straight on, down dip, to track parallel to road. Keep straight on.

6km **Urbanizacion de Santiago**
(1215)
Accommodation:
A new development whose best feature is the swimming pool at the Hostel de Montico (free to guests, otherwise an entrance charge, including hire of compulsory cap ('gorro')); rooms not cheap. Two other hostels here but next village a much nicer place to stay.
Directions:
Continue on road.

2km to **Villadangos del Paramo**
(1217)
This is an ancient village of Roman origin. In 1111 a battle is supposed to have taken place here between the troops of Alfonso of Aragon and the troops of his wife, Dona Urraca of Leon. There was a pilgrim hospital in the calle Real. The church of Santiago has two sculptured scenes above the door depicting the battle of Clavijo. A picturesquely dressed figure of Santiago Matamoros adorns the main altarpiece. .
Accommodation: Fonda Avenida on left on main road is friendly and good value. Also Bar Avenida in village not far from refuge.
Refuge: excellent, new municipal refuge at entrance to village, with hot water, kitchen (with pans), showers and bunks. Water may be turned off in summer from 4 till 8pm and all night. Charge of 2 or 3 Euros. Ask at pharmacy for the key.
Directions:
Cross road at entrance to village (refuge in former school on right). Fork right and enter village. Turn left at end to return briefly to main road. Fork left off it onto a track parallel to road. Follow as far as is practicable and rejoin road to walk on hard shoulder. You can't avoid this section. All the land to left and right of the road is criss-crossed by canals, dykes and deep irrigation channels. Continue to San martin del Camino.

4km to **San Martin del Camino**
(1221)
Small shop, 2 bars. No accommodation.
Directions:
Keep straight on. Shortly after leaving village cross road and fork right onto track parallel to road. At farm, veer slightly right, to pass it (on your left). Veer left again to follow track parallel to road. Keep straight. After 2km, the track forks away from the road. Turn left, cross bridge over dyke and return to road over crash barrier.

Go straight. 1.5km before Hospital de Orbigo, opposite a gravel works, turn right down a lane. Follow path through fields to Hospital de Orbigo, veering left at fork into the Calle Orbigo along the river. Turn left and cross the bridge over the river into the town. Continue as described on p180 from "Hospital de Orbigo".

B.   Country route via VILLAR DE MAZARIFE
This is somewhat sparsely way marked but is easy enough to follow.
Accommodation:
Two bars, bakery and food shop. Refuge. c/Corujo. Six rooms, kitchen, bath.
Turn left and veer left up side of wall uphill. keep straight on ahead. Join minor road coming from back right and keep straight on along it. Ignore next left turn, keep straight on downhill and go under road to enter Fresno del Camino.

3.5km to **Fresno del Camino**
Fountain.
Directions:
Keep straight on ahead uphill (unmarked bar in social club on right) on road marked "Oncina de la Valdoncina,2.3km". Go downhill, cross minor railway line, bridge over stream (probably dry, small fountain/water supply to left) and enter village of

Oncina del la Valdoncina.

2.3km **Oncina del la Valdoncina**
Directions:
Veer right then left uphill and keep straight on stony track (sign to "Chozos de Abajo,5km"). Continue uphill to open plateau, fork and then veer left. Continue ahead on open plateau land, more or less flat, ignoring turns to left and right. Cross minor road and enter Chozos de Abajo.

5km to **Chozos de Abajo**
Bar(meals), camping.
Keep straight on(right) on Calle Real (signed "Villar de Mazarife,4km"). Turn left and then right in village, cross bridge and keep straight on UMUR, ignoring turns to Villar de Mazarife.

4km to **Villar de Mazarife**
2 bars (neither does food), shop.
Directions:
Continue to Plaza Mediovilla and continue ahead along Calle Camino to road (Carretera Valcabo). Cross it and keep straight on (signposted "Villavente 9.3km") on minor tarred road, past sports ground (left). Keep straight on.
The paramo is almost completely flat, with cornfields, sunflowers, irrigation channels and the occasional tree. The Montes de Leon is visible from your right. Few way marks in this area. Continue straight ahead.
After 4-5km cross a minor road and continue ahead on what has now become a UMUR, turning left at small junction of similar tracks 100m later. Cross bridge over canal, veer right and keep straight on, ignoring turns to left or right. After 2km cross bridge over a large canal and then a road and keep straight on again into Villavante.

9km to **Villavante**
Bar. Bakery.

Directions:
Turn right into village at junction with tarred road and then left into Calle Santa Maria. Turn right after junction with the Calle Pradico and veer left into another street. Turn left again at bar down Calle Iglesia.
Pass church (on your right) and keep straight on, forking left down side of huge water tower.
Cross bridge over railway line (a notice at start says "Hospital de Orbigo,3.5km"). Turn left along minor road at end of bridge, continue on UMUR after last house, along side of railway track on your left.) Veer right towards Hospital de Orbigo (visible ahead).
Keep straight on for 2km, cross minor road, continue ahead (still on UMUR). Approx. 600m later reach minor road (fountain on right), passing between factory buildings. Turn right, cross main road (N120) carefully and continue ahead on Avenida de la Constitucion into Hospital de Orbigo.

7km **Hospital de Orbigo**
(819m) (1228)
Small town, with shops, fonda, restaurant, campsite, 2 fountains.
The river Orbigo is famous for some memorable battles : Suevos and Visigoths (456), Moors and Christians in the area of Alfonso III. The bridge is one of the most outstanding on the Camino. Its greatest fame came in the Holy Year 1434, with the exploits of the knight of Leon, Don Suero de Quinones. In love with a scornful lady, he promised to defend the Passage, or bridge, in a series of jousting tournaments, challenging any knights in Europe who wanted to accept, and committing himself to fight, with nine other knights, until 300 lances were broken. The jousts began on 10 July and lasted 30 days. The fame of the affair spread all over Europe and found its way into literature.

The champions, having happily finished their defence of the bridge (to which was given the title of "Honroso" or "Honourable"), made their way to Compostela to give thanks to the Apostle and to deposit in his reliquary a gold necklace. This still adorns the processional bust of St James the Less, which comes from San Isidoro in Leon.

Accommodation:
Refuge: Parish house behind church. 3-16 Euros. Municipal (20) in grounds of campsite, hot water, showers, kitchen. 3 Euros. Not recommended for women travellers.
Hostal Suero de Quinones, tel: 987 38 82 38 Rooms 68 Euros.
Hostal Kanguro Australiano. tel: 987 38 90 31. Rooms 45 Euros.
La Trucha Restaurant , Flamingo and La Isla serve meals for 10 Euros.
Campsite: Suero de Quinones has all facilities including a swimming pool. Open from June to September.

Directions:
Cross Roman bridge and continue ahead, passing Casa Consistorial (right, fountain opposite on left), church of Santa Maria (right) and keep straight on down main street to end of town (down the Calle Camino de Santiago). At the crossroads with an UMUR at the end you again have two options, either

a) keep straight on (way marked) to continue on the road route to Astorga or

b) (also way marked) turn right for an alternative country route as far as San Justo de la Vega (the one described here).

Keep straight on along minor road to Villares de Orbigo.

2km to **Villares de Orbigo**
(919m) (1230)

Directions:
Ignore turns to left and right. Enter village, turn left then right, then veer right, (past lavadero). Veer left and then turn right onto road, cross it (and canal) and keep straight on. After 200m turn left up junction with green lane. keep straight on for 1km and join road again. Turn right to village of Santibanez de Valdeiglesias.

2km to **Santibanez de Valdeiglesias**
(845m) (1232)

Enter village down Camino Villares and continue ahead down Calle Real then turn right up Calle Carromonte Alto and keep straight on, uphill all the time, into open country. At top of hill descend, taking left fork, past large sandstone quarry to left. Descend to wide shallow valley (watch out for way marks on the ground) and keep straight on ahead up other side, taking right hand fork part way up. Keep straight and take left at next fork, uphill all the time.

At top of the hill join track coming from back left and keep straight on downhill ahead. Take right hand fork (four options to left) and go uphill under trees to open plateau. (HT cables ahead, woods to left). Descend to next valley (line of trees along stream) and up again to another open plateau.
At junction of similar tracks when you are level with second farm building to right veer left under electric cables (view of Astorga ahead, below), taking right hand of two forks leading to the Crucero de Santo Toribio (and splendid views of Astorga). *(Toribio, along with Genadio, both from Astorga, Isidore of Seville and Ildefonso of Toledo, was one of the four bishop saints)* This

is where this camino joins the other from Hospital de Orbigo along the road.
Go downhill ahead and 200m later turn right onto section of old main road which then leads to the new one. Continue along it into San Justo de la Vega.

8km to **San Justo de La Vega**
Bars, shop, hostel.
Church with old tower but very modern windows and brick nave.
Accommodation :
At the Hostel Ideal, with immaculate rooms and kindly people (double 25 Euros, plus 2 Euros for bath).
Directions:
Continue through village and out along main road until you have crossed the road bridge over the river Tuerto. Turn right 100m after bend onto UMUR marked "merendero" (ie.picnic area). Turn left along a shaded lane parallel to the road. Follow this for 2km past field, factory and another field until you cross an old three-arch bridge over a small canal. Turn left onto UMUR and keep straight on to main road. Turn right along it, cross two level crossings. Turn right along this road, cross two more level crossings, and proceed uphill into town. Turn right to visit cathedral

5km to **Astorga**
(869m) (1245)
The first city, or pre-Roman "Asturica", was a camp belonging to the Amacos, then the centre of operations of Augustus, from whom it received the name "Augusta", and became the nexus of communications and administration from which departed nine roads.

It was an Episcopal see from the very beginnings of Christianity in Spain. The walled part of the city dates from Roman times. It was repopulated by settlers from the Bierzo in the middle of the ninth century, but it was from the tenth onwards that it began to develop under the influence of the pilgrimage.

Astorga is the meeting point of two pilgrimage routes: the Camino Frances and the Via de Plata. From here too, routes departed to Foncebadon and Manzanal. If we go by the records, Astorga was the locality in which, after Burgos, the most pilgrim hospitals were founded: twenty-two.

Astorga has had three cathedrals ; the existing one, begun in 1471, combines the gothic, renaissance and baroque styles, superimposed one upon another. With three aisles and graceful vaulting, it houses a singular sixteenth century altarpiece by Gaspar Becerra and a Flemish style choir, probably by the same artist. Among its sculptural treasures the following are outstanding: the Virgen de la Majestad (XI century Romanesque), the Inmaculada by Gregorio Fernandez; and the pulpit and choir stalls, probably also the work of Becerra. A relief over one door represents the foundation of the See of Astorga by St.James and St Paul. There is also, very high up on the left-hand side, a sculptured panel representing Christ entrusting the work of evangelising Spain to St James

The Cathedral Museum is in the cloister, with notable collections

of Romanesque statuary, reliquaries and metalwork dating from the twelfth to the eighteenth centuries. In the same plaza as the cathedral stands the Hospital of San Juan, founded in the twelfth century to minister to pilgrims walking to Compostela, and rebuilt in the eighteenth century. Tradition has it that St Francis of Assisi slept here in the course of his pilgrimage. To the east is the Episcopal Palace, a work designed and begun by Antonio Gaudi (1889) and finished by Ricardo Guereta. It never became the residence of a bishop, since from the beginning it served to house the Museum "de los Caminos", so called because it brings together objects from different routes that meet here: Roman roads, Jacobean routes, and the road through the Maragateria – together with related historical objects and works of art. There are many Roman and medieval epigraphs and statuary from the school of Astorga (XIII to XVIII centuries), panels by Berruguete, and other pieces of interest.

The plaza de Espana is home to the Ayuntamiento, with its baroque façade (XVII century) and its curious clock, a piece of artistry known all over Europe, and devised by Bartolome Fernandez.

Other sites to visit are the Monumento de los Sitios, the Roman Ermigastula, the ramparts, and the churches of Fatima, San Francisco, San Bartolome, and the convent of Santa Clara (gothic), Santa Marta and the monastery of Sancti Spiritus (baroque). If you are interested in parchments and other documents, you can visit the Diocesan Archive behind the cathedral.

Buses to Leon, Ponferrada and Villafranca del Bierzo. Tourist Office opposite Cathedral.

Between Astorga and Ponferrada the camino passes through the isolated area of the Maragateria (as far as the Cruz de Ferro) and then into the Bierzo region, which continues until you leave the province of Leon and enter Galicia. For many people this is one of the most beautiful stretches of the camino, most of it in the Montes de Leon, but as there are few villages and few bars or shops along the way it is advisable to carry a certain amount of food and water. Since the route is also quite high (the Cruz de Ferro is at 1504m) warm clothing is needed, even in summer.

Much of the Camino between Astorga and Molinaseca is in fact on the road but it is very quiet and there is very little traffic.

Accommodation:

The Hotel Gaudi is the place to stay if you want centrally located luxury. Otherwise the Hostel Santa Ana, triangular pale yellow building on the way in is handy, but overpriced for what it offers. La Peseta, Plaza de San Bartolome (near the town hall) is acceptable but no longer cheap; beware of disco opposite and late August fiesta. Pension Garcia, on right near town hall at Bajada Postigo 5, is traditional pilgrim place, but rooms may be occupied in the week by people working in Astorga. Two hostels on the main N6 road, just past the pilgrim road out of town and therefore handy for the following day, are: Hostel Gallego (35 Euros for dinner, wine b & b for 1 person) and the cheaper Hostel Coruna nearby; this can be very noisy at night. Even cheaper is the Hostel San Narciso opposite (1500 for single with bath) - noisy but adequate. Restaurante Triton, General Mola 12 has good food. Also Bar Cubasol. Sr. Ovalle 8 (off Plaza Mayor) whose restaurant is used by many pilgrims. Gaudi and Peseta are good but expensive. Bar la Paloma has good food. Bar /Rest Jaun Luis c/San Pedro 49. Casa Maragata. c/Husar Tiburcio 2, serves typically local food.

Refuge: Colegio Santa Maria Madre de Ia Iglesia, 1/2km from town on western road to Sanabria; large complex of red brick buildings, which is a school for young people with learning difficulties. Ask at first building on the right where refuge is round the back in off-peak months (has hot showers). In July/August they use the gymnasium, (no mattresses, but showers). No kitchen at any time. Charge of 2 to 3 Euros. Ring first to check: 61.59.76. Cycle Repairs: Ciclos Lob, Avda de las Murallas 48, tel.(987)61.85.81. Rebaque Gonzalez, Plaza Lorenzo Lafuente 2, tel.(987)61.59.45.

There are some bars and fountains. A morning start from Astorga is sensible and water and a small amount of food should be carried as a precaution. Warm clothes may be needed even in the summer months. The highest point is 1500 metres.

Directions:

To take your leave of Astorga, turn left at traffic lights on main road out of Astorga to the west onto minor road signposted "Santa Colomba de Somoza" and "Castrillo de los Polvazares". Go straight to Valdeviejas, passing a memorial sign (left) to "peregrinos identes" and an old people's complex (left). Pass the Ermita Ecco Homo (left). Either keep straight on road itself or along a track beside it as far as the bridge over the river Jerga and turn to the road. Continue to village of Murias de Rechivaldo.

4km to **Murias de Rechivaldo**
(882m) (1249)
Bar, meson. Fork left onto a track between two trees just past the village name sign and pass along to the side of the village to its left. Enter street (Camino de Santiago) and continue along to the end, when it becomes a track leading to open country.
Accommodation:
An excellent new 'hospederia' opened last year, just south of the church. Rooms and food both good value though not cheap. There are also 3 mesons (restaurants):Meson del Arriero, the first of the three, on the right as you come into the village; lunch starts at 2 and consists of a 'cocido Maragato' (pork and bean stew

characteristic of the area) which costs 14 Euros for a full meal. Meson Ia Magdalena, on left further into the village serves a similar lunch at 2.30. There is a 3rd meson, name unknown, which only cooks meals ordered in advance. 'Bocadillos' are available earlier in the day. Restaurante Antonio and Meson El Rancho serve good meals.

Directions:
Follow this track straight on for 2km, until you reach the road. Cross over and keep straight on ahead (signposted "El Ganso5") and keep straight on to village of Santa Catalina de Somoza.

5km to **Santa Catalina de Somoza**
(997m) (1254)
Like many of the villages of the Maragateria the Camino goes through the middle of the village on the Calle Real.
Refuge: (34) Key from Bar Peregrino. No kitchen but hot water. Bar Peregrino on main road Open only in summer. .

Directions:
Fork right at entrance to village along lane towards church and keep straight on along Calle Real. Rejoin road at large green wooden wayside cross and keep straight on along road to El Ganso.

4km to **El Ganso**
(1013m) (1258)
 A tiny, windswept village, with an ancient church dedicated to Santiago. Its porch offers shelter from rain or sun. Exterior chapel of Christ of the Pilgrims would have been available for medieval pilgrims, but is now kept locked.
Two bars: the eccentric Cowboy Bar in the centre of the village and a new one on the main tarmac road run by Manuel and Pilar.
Refuge: (20) No water. Keys from Caferino Pastor. Cowboy Bar and La Barraca Bar. Open only in summer.

Directions:
Fork right at entrance to village along lane (village to your left). Keep straight on and turn left back onto road at church. Proceed

straight along road, pass a turning to "Rabanal Viejo" after 3km at the Puente Panote, and continue to Rabanal del Camino.

6km to **Rabanal del Camino**
(1149m) (1264)
2 bars (meals available at both, one has rooms), fountain.
End of the ninth stage in Aimery Picaud's guide. Ermita del Santo Cristo at entrance to village, church of San Jose and parish church of Santa Maria. Today the population is only twenty-seven, except in summer when migrants return for their holidays, but in former times it was an important pilgrim halt and considerably larger, as the presence of three churches testifies.

Accommodation:
Refuge: Refugio Gaucelmo (40) near Santa Maria. hot water, kitchen, showers, salon and library. Nuestra Senora del Pilar (52) In the village square. Kitchen, hot showers. Rooms 10 Euros. Municipal refugeis also in main square. No hot water. For keys orange house upstairs. Hosteria Refugo tel: 987 69

12 74. Double 50 Euros. Single 35 Euros. Chonina has a small number of rooms where people can stay (not in August). She also serves excellent food, preferably ordered in advance (certainly for groups), and her famous pilgrim soup. The Bar/Meson Refugio, on the Calle Real, near the church and the new refuge, is a larger establishment that also has some rooms. The owner, Antonio, is helpful to pilgrims and sells them food for the next day's walk. Both bars have telephones.

Refuges: two refuges. The Refugio Gaucelmo (30) opposite Santa Maria was converted from the derelict parish house in 1991 by the Confraternity of St James and the local El Bierzo Association. A typical Maragato house, it has a large upstairs dormitory with bunk beds and 3 smaller family rooms, showers and a balcony for drying washing. Downstairs is the kitchen (with pans), 'salon', library, barn, patio and large garden. Hot water is available in months other than July/August; water is short in the village in August. Doors locked 11pm. Open April to late October, with wardens there full-time. Preference given to walkers with no back-up transport. No fixed charge but donations requested. The other (municipal) refuge is in the square, key from Chonina; it has fewer facilities, but is useful for groups and the overflow from the Gaucelmo.

Directions:
Turn right off road after church (left) to enter village. Pass churches of San Jose and Santa Maria and meson and keep straight on green lane for 1 km to rejoin road again. Stick to this road. (Fountain to right of road after 2km at KM25, icy cold water). Continue your climb and advance towards village of Foncebadon.

5km to **Foncebadon**
(1495m) (1269)
A seemingly abandoned village although there are still two residents left. Early in the 12th century the hermit, Gaucelmo, received permission from the Bishop of Astorga to build a church, a hospital and a hospice for pilgrims. The new refuge at Rabanal is named after him.
Directions:

Fork left off road, enter village and continue to end. Go straight, passing ruined church and rejoin road after 1km. Turn left and 300m after reach the Cruz de Ferro.

1.5km to **Cruz de Ferro**

Famous Cruz de Ferro (Iron Cross) stands on a great pile of stones. Traditionally each pilgrim adds one as they pass. There is a small chapel nearby, built in 1982, the last Holy Year but one. The Cruz de Ferro is at 1504m, just short of the highest point of the whole route, 1517m, at a point between Manjarin and El Acebo.

Directions:
RJ: turn right off road between twentyfirst and twentysecond snow pole on road after passing the cross. If you miss it, continue along the road to rejoin the Camino at the entrance to Foncebadon.

Keep straight on road, passing highest point of the entire route (at 1517m) to another almost abandoned village of Manjarin.

3.5km to **Manjarin**

Abandoned village, but with very small, simple refuge.

Directions:
Continue on road for 2km, pass turning to military base (visible on hill above road, with radar, etc) and keep straight on. Mountain ranges visible. After 1-2km watch out for a turning off the road to the right, 200m after road KM37 and 100m after an iron cross on right. Fork right off road which ascends up between two small hills; this avoids some of the road's many hairpins and does away with a long section off the road, which you rejoin on the other side (good view of Ponferrada ahead). [RJ: turn left uphill , near drain, before road veers right.].

400m further on, at sign marked "Ruta peatonal", fork left off road onto foot path going downhill below the road (on your right). Continue, descending steeply, until abruptly, below, you reach the slate-roofed village of El Acebo.

7km to **El Acebo**
(1156m) (1281)

Fountain on roadside as you leave the foot path and 2 others in village. Bar. Another village which formerly had a pilgrim hospital, a single long, narrow street whose old houses have overhanging balconies at first floor level and outside staircases. Their slate roofs are a sudden change from the red pantiles encountered up to now. Church has statue of Santiago Peregrino.

Accommodation:
Refuge: Municipal (12) Cold water for baths. Key from bar. Refugo Taberna de Jose (50) One hot shower 5 Euros. Key at Jose`s taberna. Refugo Meson El Acebo. (28) 5 Euros. hot showers and modern facilities. Refugio Meson el Acebo in at the centre of the village. Good meals at Taberna de Jose..
Cyclists should note that from Foncebadon to Molinaseca, and especially from El Acebo, the road descends steeply, with some blind bends to negotiate. Check your brakes are in good order and then enjoy the views and the perfumed air.

Directions:
Keep straight on through village, past ermita and cemetery and a memorial in the form of an iron bicycle sculpture to a German pilgrim killed there in 1987 as he was cycling to Santiago. Continue on road. 1km before the next village of Riego de Ambros, visible ahead, watch out for a turning to left of road, just before a bend, onto a foot path below the road. Follow this down to the village.
In the section from Foncebadon to Riego de Ambros there are a lot of wayside crosses with scallop shells below : memorials to pilgrims who died en route?

2km to **Riego de Ambros**
(920m)(1283)
A slightly bigger village with 2 bars, both good, and a shop. The one on the path out of the village (by the road) is the Meson Ruta Santiago and more accessible to cyclists and motorists.

Directions:
Enter village, follow street straight on (downhill all the time) and then turn right down a grassy lane. Continue downhill through trees, for 1 km (straight all the time). Join a farm track. Join a

road a few metres further on and turn left. 80 m after this, turn right off the road to a track. Keep straight, fork right downhill and zigzag down to clearing in a wood with enormous chestnut trees. Go straight downhill. After a while, the path remains level. The land falls away into a valley so that you are actually walking quite high up in an area perfumed with cistus, a bush with incense like fragrance. Track veers right and eventually descends to the road. 100m before this, turn left along track coming from right. You can either turn left to road (at bridge) or continue for a short while longer up hill to right on path, joining road further down at large wayside cross. Continue down the road to large village of Molinaseca.

Note:
Walkers should take care from Riego to Molinaseca, for two reasons:
1) a local prankster from time to time turns one of the marker stones around. When you cross the road there should be a big marker
stone showing the path on the other side.

2) the path is not always easy to follow and there are one or two very steep descents.

5km to **Molinaseca**
(595m)(1288)
A pretty village a few km before the industrial city of Ponferrada. Near the Romanesque bridge on the way in the river has been dammed to make an excellent spot for swimming.

Accommodation:
Refuge: (30) on Ponferrada Road 500m out of village. Showers, hot water, kitchen. Prefrence is given to walkers. 5 Euros. Key from Alfredo near Bodega La Rana. Hostel el Palacio tel:987 45 30 94. Double 35 Euros. La Casa del Reloj tel: 987 45 31 24. Double 40 Euros. Posada de Muriel tel: 987 45 32 01. Double 90 Euros. Meals: Meson del Puente and Rest. Azar c/El Palacio 10.

Directions:
Enter village passing Ermita de las Angustias (right), partly set in the cliffs, and cross the Romanesque Puente de las Peregrinos over the river Meruelboo. Continue along the Calle Real (the main street). This runs into the main road. Keep straight until you reach tennis court on your right. Turn off road to right, turn left along a lane parallel to road. Go straight as it passes behind the houses on the main road, cross a minor road and continue straight on uphill along the side of fields. Rejoin road at the top of the hill, just before crossroads.

At the top of the hill, the road goes downhill (good view of Ponferrada ahead, church tower to left hand side is Basilica de la Encina). 100 m later you can choose one of two routes into Ponferrada (both way marked), right or left. The right hand route is slightly shorter, much of it on a busy road; the left hand route is slightly longer and is not particularly scenic. However, it takes you on quieter and calmer roads with substantially less traffic. There is more shade too.

LH ROUTE VIA **CAMPO** :

Fork left down minor road and keep straight on (left) for 50m down earth track. Fork left 100m later downhill on earth/grassy track/lane. This climbs uphill going over a stream. Keep straight on (uphill) at crossing with similar track (vines to your left)[RJ: keep straight on at right fork uphill.)

Descend downhill again. Approx.1.5km after making your left hand/right hand choice you are in the village of Campo.

3km to **Campo**
Directions:
Take right hand fork down Calle Real (lined with old houses on both sides) (Stone sitting area at junction) [RJ: fork right at 2 earth tracks at top of Calle Real.] There's an eighteenth-century church to left.

At small plaza at the bottom of the Calle Real continue along left hand of two roads (no name at start). This is part gravelled and part tarred. KS0 (left) at junction with Calle de los Mesones passing through waste ground, sports ground (to right), past rubbish tip, slaughterhouse and large factory. Go straight to "stop" sign. [RJ: left Fork at junction.] 500m further on road runs into a main road emerging from back left. Bar at crossing. [RJ: Take left hand for marked "Los Barrios".]

Continue 100m to next junction (shop to the left) and turn right. Cross the medieval Puente Mascaron over the Rio Boeza to enter Ponferrada. Turn left on other side up Calle Camino Bajo de San Andres. Go under railway line and uphill. At the junction at the top you can choose your way, both are marked.

a) Right along Calle el Camino Jacobeo, turn left 50m later and right into Calle Hospital. (b) Keep straight on (left) along Calle Buenavista. Take right almost immediately along Calle Hospital, the fifteenth century Hospital de la Reina at No28. Turn left at top, right up Calle Gil y Carrasco (up the side of castle). The Tourist Office is on left. Follow uphill into the Plaza Virgen de la Encina.

Right hand (Road) ROUTE :
Keep straight on road for 1.5km. Veer right at fork by furniture

warehouse, just before road KM54. Continue downhill, cross bridge over Rio Boeza and shortly afterwards take path beside road on left hand side. Veer slightly left ,off road, behind factory 500m later and keep straight on along lane between low walls with fields on either side following HT lines. After1km fork right uphill, cross bridge over railway line, veer left along cemetery wall and past entrance to road. Turn left, and at crossing with small roundabout, take Calle del Pregonero. Keep straight along Calle El Templo to castle, and then up Calle Gil y Carrasco to Plaza de la Encina.

8km to **Ponferrada**
(543m) (1296)
Large industrial town at the junction of the rivers Boeza and Sil. The town takes its name from the iron bridge over the Sil. Nowadays a metal bridge is not a novelty, but was something to marvel at when it was built at the end of the twelfth century. Unsurprisingly, the area is rich in iron.
The new part of the town is on the west side of the river Sil, the old part on the east.
The city probably dates from pre-Roman times, although its site was abandoned. Only the places of greatest historical interest will be singled out here, but your visit to the city should not be rushed.
The Templar's Castle : Fernando II of Leon repopulated the town and gave it to the Order of the Temple (Templars) in 1185, although they were expelled from it in 1312. This military fortress is still a thrilling site today, with its different architectural styles and periods (XII and XIII centuries, with elements from the XVth). For a time it belonged to the Counts of Lemos, and to the Catholic Monarchs. It served as a fortress, palace and monastery. Of the part that constituted the monastery hardly anything remains. In 1924 the castle was declared a National Monument.

The Basilica de Nuestra Senora de la Encina: Shortly after the arrival of the Templars, there occurred an apparition of The Virgin in a nearby oak wood. Devotion to the Virgen de la Encina (holm-oak) spread through the district. In 1958 the Virgin was declared Patroness of the Bierzo and the church was elevated to the status of a basilica. The existing edifice dates from the sixteenth century. The niche that holds the Virgin's statue is in the churrigueresque style.

San Andreas, a seventeenth century baroque church, has an altarpiece in the same style and a fourteenth century figure of Christ known as the "Cristo del castillo".

The Conceptionist monastery was built in 1542. The Ayuntamiento belongs to the end of the seventeenth century and the Torre del Reloj to the sixteenth.

Excursions:
The tenth century mozarabic church of **Santo Tomas de las Ollas** stands in a suburb of Ponferrada. It has a single rectangular nave and an oval apse with rounded Moorish arches supported on square granite pillars. **Santa Maria de Vizbayo** is on the other side of the river Boeza and is Romanesque,

dating from the eleventh century. **Santiago de Penalba** is a tenth century mozarabic church with a divided main door with Moorish arches and an alfiz, or ornamental frame, on marble columns with splendid capitals. It is a National Monument, but deserves better care. A few kilometres away stands the monastery of San Pedro de Montes, founded by San Fructuoso in the seventh century and rebuilt in the eleventh. It is mainly Romanesque with asturian style capitals, but it also possesses mozarabic and neoclassical features. Known as the "Spanish Tebaid", this famous and very ancient monastery is today in ruined and shameful condition.

Accommodation:
Hostel Santa Cruz (T: 987-41 63 51), calle Marcello Macias 4, off the avda de Espana, is recommended (25 Euros for single with bath). Hotel de Madrid (T:987-41 15 50), avda de Ia Puebla, is a traditional hotel that is very good value (40 Euros for a double room) and helpful with bikes; its restaurant is also reasonable with a menu at 9 Euros. Bar/restaurant Gundin, on corner of Isidoro Rueda and Antolin Lopez (for people at the Hostel Santa Cruz) Pizzeria Trastevere, Plaza del Ayuntamiento (old town) and Bar Acapulco near La Encina. Hotel San Miguel, tel: 987 42 47 00. Double 48 Euros. Single 28 Euros. Menu for 12 Euros.

Refuge: in 1993 the refuge was a sports pavilion some 30 minutes' walk from the Plaza de Ia Encina and not on the Camino No bunks, floor space only. For 1994 enquire at Tourist Office or at church of La Encina.

Campsite: El Bierzo at Carracedelo, which is signposted off the southern loop of the NVI, about 12km west of Ponferrada on the way to Villafranca. Closer to Cacabelos (see below) but serves whole Ponferrada/Villafranca area. Class II site, open June to end of September. Bar and restaurant but no shop.

Cycle Repairs: Bicicletas Marques, avda Portugal 54, tel. (987) 41.22.26; Rodriguez Guerrero, avda Asturias 164, tel.41.63.61; Roia Babbis, avda Espana 50, tel. 41.59.56.

Directions:
The exit from Ponferrada is unattractive and rather tardily way marked. From the Plaza de la Encina, next to the Basilica, veer left across square and down Calle El Ranadero (stepped street).

Turn left at bottom, cross river and take second right down Calle Rio Urdiales. This veers left into a big square/parking lot. Go straight, and at end, turn right down wide tree-lined avenue (Avenida del Sacramento). This veers left, rising uphill to Plaza Lutero King which is surrounded by big blocks of flats with a back drop of an enormous slag heap.

Turn right (way mark) along Avenida de la Libertad (slag heap on your left). Keep straight, ignore misleading way mark near right hand fork leading to a disused factory. 400m later, turn left at junction in front of electricity headquarters into tree-lined road. Ignore first left fork, keep straight on and turn right at end, then left, left again. Keep straight on and turn right alongside the church of Santa Maria de Compostilla. There's a modern statue to left opposite entrance. In the entrance arcade, you will also encounter murals painted in the 1993 Holy Year.

Cross road, continue down IV Avenida. There's a private house on your left with two very tall chimneys. A stork's nest rests on top one of these chimneys. Go through a residential area with numbered, not named streets. Turn left then right towards 3a Transversal past tennis courts (on left), the Ermita (not a church), Nuestra Senora de Compostilla (modern mural at end) and modern cruceiro. St. James the pilgrim is on one side, the Virgin and Child on the other.

Keep straight on towards new housing, keep straight on under crossing of two sets of HT cables (waste ground to right). The main road leading to NVI is visible to the right.

Keep straight on at junction with Calle Santa Rosa and continue on Calle de Finisterre which becomes a lane (church bell tower visible). Keep straight on ignoring turnings (vines to your left). Go under the NVI and continue on road ahead. At end, you pass church of Columbrianos. (left)

3km to **Columbrianos**
(1299/)
The Church's large covered porch with thoughtful seating provides a welcome rest. You get an interesting view of the mountains into the bargain.
Directions:

Keep straight downhill (Calle El Teso). Cross bridge over railway line, go down steps at bend, cross road and continue down Calle La Iglesia (unmarked at the beginning). Fountain and seats in front of the Centre Civico.

Join Calle Real comes from your left. Continue on it, veer left at chapel (bar to right) down Calle San Blas (again unmarked at start) with fields on either side. Cross minor railway line and keep straight for 2km, ignoring turns to left or right. Road joins from back left [RJ: left fork-earth road], which becomes Calle Paraiso in Fuentesnuevas.

3km to **Fuentesnuevas**
(1302)
Directions:
Emerge at crossing, continue on Calle Real (bar on right, cruceiro to left) in village and keep straight passing church on your right and continue through fields for 1.5km until track joins road from back left in Camponaraya.

2km to **Camponaraya**
490m (1304)
A long, straggling village with shops, bars, bank.
There is also a cycle repair shop here: Guerrero Valtuille, avda Francisco Sobrin 14, tel. (987) 46.34.97.
Directions:
Turn right onto road [RJ: turn left at house no.337] and continue through village past church and over Rio Naraya. At the end (1km) the NVI veers right (wine cooperative to your left). Keep straight (left) uphill on earth road /track through vines.
From here you can you get a splendid view of the mountains of the El Bierzo region. The Camino leads through orchards and vines for much of the time.
Continue, ignoring turnings, until you cross the road again shortly before the entrance to Cacabelos.

4km to **Cacabelos**

(486m) (1309/)
Attractive village surrounded by orchards and vineyards. Shops, fonda, bank. Swimming area in the river.
The first bar/restaurant that walkers encounter, La Moncloa, has pleasant outdoor eating area; they may offer a free drink to pilgrims. Otherwise food is good but expensive. Ask here about the refuge.

The church of Santa Maria dates from the sixteenth century, with vestiges of its twelfth century predecessor. It has a figure of Christ (XVI century) and a small stone statue of the Virgin (XIII century).
The neoclassical sanctuario de la Quinta Angustia (XVIII century) was already documented as existing in the thirteenth century. Nearby is a pilgrim hospital, one of five which existed in the area.
The Archaeological Museum contains interesting objects from the surrounding area.
On leaving the town note old wine press to right hand side of road.
Excursions:
Towards the north lies Vega de Espinareda, with its Benedictine monastery of San Andres. One kilometre to the south, the Cistercian monastery of Carracedo, with interesting Romanesque remains, and the Romanesque church of Carracedelo.

Accommodation:
Fonda Miralrio, the last house on the right before the river (and through the long village) is reported clean and comfortable. Bar with 'camas' on left near the church. Mes6n El Apostol, Santa Maria 27, is half-way down village, on the right before market and church, and may offer wine and coffee free to pilgrims. Bar El Molino offers 'camas' and son of the house speaks English. For greater comfort the Hotel/Restaurante El Gato almost outside the western end of the village (Antigua Carretera Madrid-Coruna) is recommended. Prices for rooms not known. but excellent food (menu at 13 Euros) and swimming pool

.

Refuge: Casa Parroqulal offers small refuge.

Campsite: the El Bierzo (see under Ponferrada) which is about 5km south of Cacabelos very near Villmartin de la Abadia. Bar and restaurant; no shop. Swimming in the river but keep an eye on possessions.

Directions:

Go downhill into the town. Keep straight down main street, pass fifteenth-century Capilla de San Roque (right) and continue down pedestrianised street. If you turn left you emerge into a tree-lined square with seats, shade, shops. Pass to left of church and go straight down Calle de las Angustias. Proceed, cross bridge over river and stick to main road.

Go for 2km past hamlet of Pierros (fountain close to bus shelter) and two other unmarked paths. Immediately past a bridge, 200m after a signpost to "Valtuille". Just after a stone house (right) and a meson/sidreria turn right off the road and veer left to a track through vines, parallel to road and narrowing greatly. Keep straight on (avoid more obvious left fork) down other side of hill, sloping to road.

Turn right (tractor opening in hedge by roadside 20m to your left). Take left at the bottom up a clear track going uphill diagonally right from the road. Stick to this track until you reach the Romanesque church of Santiago (left), by cemetery on the outskirts of Villafranca del Bierzo.

8km to **Villafranca del Bierzo**
(511m) (1317)

One of the most attractive towns on the Camino. Nearly every pilgrim spends a night here before going up to El Cebrero. Tourist Office (summer only) in the Alameda Alta, past church of San Nicolas.

A community of French immigrants, "Villa Franca", was founded here in the eleventh century. Later, monks from Cluny arrived, who built the church of Nuestra Senora de Cluniaco. The town was at first administered by the king; later it passed into the hands of the Osorio family. In 1486 the marquisate of Villafranca was created. It suffered attacks and occupation during the War of Independence. In 1822, when the province of

El Bierzo came into being, Villafranca became the capital and remained so until 1833.

The twelfth century church of Santiago is Romanesque and stands right on the Camino. Its north door, the "Puerta del mPerdon", is handsome , with illustrative capitals. Pilgrims who reached this point and found themselves unable to continue their journeys gained the same pardon and spiritual benefits at this church as they would Have gained had they reached Compostela.

The church of San Francisco faces that of Santiago on the right, in the upper part of the town. St Francis himself is said to have founded it. It has a Romanesque door (XIII century), an isle with an interesting mudejar coffered ceiling and a fourteenth century gothic chancel.

The sixteenth century collegiate church of Santa Maria is built on a plain devised by Gil de Hontanon. Only half of it was ever constructed. It has a handsome altarpiece depicting the Trinity (XVI century).

The Anunciada was founded as a Franciscan convent in 1606. It has an Italianate doorway and a seventeenth century altarpiece of the school of Becerra. The casket which holds the Sacrament came from Rome. The church contains the tomb of San Lorenzo of Brindisi and was the burial place of the Marquesses of Villafranca.

San Nicolas, a Jesuit monastery, is a copy of the baroque church of the Gesu in Rome and dates from the seventeenth century. It has a churrigueresque altarpiece, a baroque cloister, and an image of Cristo de la Esperanza (Hope), patron of the town. The building is administered by the Pauline Fathers, and is the monastery in which Domenico Laffi celebrated Mass.

The Hospital of Santiago is today the Colegio de la Divina Pastora. There were once five other hospitals in the town. The Castillo-Palacio de los Marqueses was begun in 1490 and lost is towers in the War of Independence.

Situated along the calle de Agua are the palaces of Torquemada and Alvarez de Toledo, and the chapel of Omanas. The writer Friar Martin Sarmiento and the poet and romantic novelist Gil y Carrasco were born in this street.

Excursions:

Towards the south lies the church of San Fiz de Visonia, the site of San Fructuoso's third monastery, built in the seventh century. It later belonged to the Order of St John of Jerusalem. Corullon, also to the south, has the Romanesque churches of San Miguel and San Esteban. The castle is fourteenth century and belonged to the Valcarce family, then the Osorio family, and finally to the marquesses of Villafranca. The spot offers a view over the Bierzo.

Accommodation:

The modern Parador Villafranca, avda Calvo Sotelo (the main road) is among the cheapest of the paradors, eg single room 50 Euros, but good value and staff helpful. Hotel San Francisco* in the main square is clean and comfortable (no restaurant). The cavernous and partly 15th c. Hostel Comerdo is good value and very cheap but no sign of life before 9.30am. Hotel La Cruce (out of town, 10-minute walk) is welcoming. At western end of town, over bridge at start of old NVI, between road and river, is the Hostel Mendez with good restaurant and reasonably priced rooms (38 Euros double, 2000 single). La Charola on the by-pass has cheap and ample food (no rooms). Near the Hostel Comerdo is the Meson Natcho, where the food is good (but tapas expensive). It is down an alley on the left going into the town, from the Comerdo; sign to it merely says Meson.

Refuge: very friendly refuge provided by Don Jesus Arias Jato and family, close to the church of Santiago. Hot showers, and hot meals provided (6 Euros) whether people stay or not. More permanent refuge currently being built. Bar, souvenirs, help provided if needed.

Cycle Repairs. Fernandez Guerra, calle Cortijo 2, tel. (987)54.00.03.

Directions:

When you leave the church of Santiago go downhill to the privately owned Castillo. Take second turn right downhill (at side of castle). Cross street, go down a flight of steps and keep straight past a small square and the "Correos" along the Calle del Agua. Turn sharp left at the bottom (Plazuela Santa Catalina), go up steps and cross the bridge over the river Burbia.

You now have three choices, all way marked: a slightly longer high level route to the right of the main road and a low level one. Both join up in Trabadelo. A longer, strenuous option passes to the left of the main road via Dragonte rejoining the other two in Herrerias.

A. ROAD ROUTE

You are strongly advised to go for the option in bad weather. Continue on the road, flat but busy. In some parts use the old sections where it has been straightened out. To do so, keep straight on along the road on the lower (left) of the two way marked routes. This leads to the exit of the road tunnel under the mountains on the way out of the town. Turn right onto main road. Keep straight on, leaving it from time to time as indicated by the yellow arrows (eg. through Pereje and 1km before Trabadelo, panaderia at end of village on right). Here the Camino takes the old route in places where the new one has been "straightened out".

Continue for 200m before you reach the Hostel Valcarce at road KM48. 200m later take the old route to your left at Portela (fountain, bar in summer). Rejoin main road. 500m after the end of this hamlet, turn left off main road to Ambasmestas, 0.5km (panaderia) and keep straight on to Vega de Valcarce.

B. HIGH-LEVEL ROUTE VIA PRADELA:

This high level route is also way marked and much quieter with the advantage of superb views on a clear day. It is much more challenging calling for a lot of stamina. It ascends very steeply and descends abruptly to Trabadelo. If you have knee problems stay away from this route. You can see the NVI below in the valley to the left most of the time.

If you decide on this option, fork right after crossing the bridge over the Burbia and go uphill between houses. This climbs steeply, levelling out from time to time before climbing again hugging the shoulder of the hillside. After 1.5km pass a grove of chestnut trees to your left, good for a break. Keep straight on (right) up narrow lane with rocky embankments on either side. These widen. Track continues to climb, levelling out with HT pylons to right hand side.

Pass under HT cables as track veers right. [View of several similar type caminos ahead: yours is the high-level one heading for a small wood on the skyline (next to further HT pylons)]. At fork 200m after passing under cables keep straight on (right) on the higher of two choices. Ignore next right hand turn and keep straight on (left) ahead. 200m later at next fork, go straight on (right) uphill, passing to right of wood (fir trees).

As you proceed this route is either level or slightly undulating with all round mountain views. After 1km pass under HT cables. [RJ: Keep straight on (left) at fork by pylon.] Ignore next left hand fork downhill to trees. Keep straight on (right). Lesser track joins from back. [RJ: keep straight on (right). Route climbs a little again (TV/radio mast above to right). [100m later minor road joins from back left : ignore RJ and keep straight on (left) ahead.

Track descends to edge of woods.
View of village of Pradela. At "U" shaped fork, you have a choice

of routes, to left *or* right, *either side of the walled field ahead. Both routes are equally attractive and both are way marked. The right hand one is slightly longer and may be muddier because of rain. Views to right hand side include a picturesque valley on other side. This takes you to Pradela (fountain, but no other facilities). The LH option is slightly shorter, with more shade and probably drier. Views to* left *over NVI.*

a) Right hand route:
Take right hand fork and keep straight on. [After 20m track joins from back right: RJ: keep straight on (right).] After 1km enter village, passing cemetery and church. Turn right in front of church. Go up flight of concrete steps (fountain at top) and left again onto road. Go straight on it until you see the right hand fork (way marked) descending off the road 400m later and continue as in option **b.**

b) LEFT HAND route:
Follow earth road to (tarmac) road, joining it shortly before entrance to village of Pradela (to your right). Turn left for 800m, veering right at bend with further choice (also way marked). Either:

- Continue left on grassy track through woods, slightly uphill. Cross small gulley, turn right and left at track. The path is not always very clear on the ground but the way marks on the trees are more helpful. This is the shortest of the three options and is relatively easy to follow as it goes in a straight line. This joins the road from Pradela (ie. from your right) at the point where you fork right off it downhill .
- OR: keep straight on road, forking right down track on right hand side just before sharp left hand bend in road.

Turn right down a track that forks right off it from Pradela and descending steeply. Pass under HT cables and rejoin road at second pylon. [RJ: turn left uphill at pylon to second track] Turn right downhill (i.e. short-cutting zigzags to Trabadelo). 20m later turn right down very steep grassy track (plastic tape way marks only). Track joins from left and then track joins from back right. [RJ: keep straight on (right).].
Rejoin road again. [RJ: take second left hand turn off road .] Turn right and follow it down to old main road [RJ: turn left at

"stop" sign and "Pradela 4" notice by quarry] at end of village of Trabadelo.

10km to **Trabadelo**
(1327)
Trabadelo was given by Alfonso III to the church of Compostela and remained in its possession from 895 until the nineteenth century. In 1703 it came under the jurisdiction of Sarracin with the right of presentation belonging to the marquis of Villafranca and that of nomination to the archbishop of Compostela. Finally, it belonged to the diocese of Lugo. Today, like the whole region around the river Valcarce, it belongs to the diocese of Astorga.

Bar, panaderia, fountain. Bar/restaurant and bar/meson 100m on other side of main road, just over the river.
Accommodation:
Nova ruta H (T: 987-54 30 81 or 987-54 32 66)
Directions:
Continue on the old road for a short distance before joining the main road. Turn right and keep straight on. Cross river Valcarce (several times) and turn right to a section of the old road. Rejoin main road, pass hostel/bar (right) at Portela and then fork left onto old road again (fountain on right, 50m later).
At a large road junction signposted "Pedrafita14" veer left down old road through small villages of Ambasmestas (fountain by Ermita) and Ambascasas. The viaduct is high above you to the right. Continue to Vega deValcarce.

C. HIGH-LEVEL ROUTE VIA DRAGONTE
This is a much longer option but rewarding in good weather. Obviously, having come a long way you have proven your fitness for this minor ordeal. There are several long climbs and descents. Make sure you have provisions and water. (there are fountains in some villages). If you are starting from Villafranca you may prefer to break your journey and sleep in Herrerias: Bar Adela at end of village does simple meals and pilgrims can

sleep on the floor.

This is not just an attractive alternative to the main camino, however, but a road used by pilgrims in the past, particularly those who were ill or with infectious diseases. The former monastery of San Fructuoso in Villar de Corrales (only the church remains today) is said to have looked after pilgrims and is on the site of a spring with healing properties. Start early in the morning.

Leave Viillafranca in the manner of the previous two options. Cross a second bridge (left, over the Rio Valcarce) and keep straight along the Calle Salvador to the NVI at the entrance to the road tunnel (bar at crossroads).

Cross the NVI and keep straight on ahead (marked "LE622 Corullon"). Fork right steeply uphill 300m later up minor tarred road marked "Dragonte 4.3". Stick to it uphill all the time, ignoring turnings till you reach the village of Dragonte.

7km **Dragonte** 900m
Directions:
Keep straight through village and continue on earth road, uphill all the time. After 2 km, turn right down grassy track just before brow of hill. There's a marker stone with conch shell to indicate turn (1090m).

You have a splendid view of the villages including Moral de Valcarce, your next port of call.

After 150m of steep descent, veering left, turn right down earth road and go straight downhill. 150 m later, fork left down a smaller track (a short cut, village to left) and then again 100m later. After 20m join asphalt road leading into Moral deValcarce.

4km **Moral de Valcarce**
Fountain at end of village. Chestnut grove at entrance. A good place for rest.
Directions:
Continue downhill and at village end, fork left downhill at

fountain and lavadero and descend down lane with concrete surface. Go down, zigzagging to valley bottom. Cross stream and old mill building on left. Useful for rest/shelter in bad weather. Keep straight to valley bottom.
Village of Villar de Corrales and church visible you on the skyline. Lane may be flooded for short distance by overflowing stream.
Keep straight (small foot path to left of stream). Veer left, slightly uphill. Track gets steeper, zigzagging. Emerge by church of San Fructuoso in village of Villar de Corrales.

5km Villar de Corrales
(1050m)
The church originally formed part of a monastery which looked after sick pilgrims, its emplacement visible on wall behind church, all that is left of former large complex. Fountain 50m later on left.
Directions:
Keep straight on (left) at fork 100m later. Continue straight on (right). Turn left at junction at top of hill and ridge. Go straight and descend via grassy road, ignoring turns to left and right. Turn left at large junction, crossing steep forest road (total absence of shade). Zigzag through quarry workings, passing workmen's huts to road below.
You can see San Fiz de Seo, to which you are heading on the other side of the road.
Turn right along road and fork left uphill (fountain on left hand side of road) to village of San Fiz do Seo.

7km to San Fiz de Seo
(650m)
Directions:
Turn left at church and go straight through village. *(Bar, unmarked, not always open, on road above you to right).*
Continue to end of village and stick to earth lane. Quarry visible to left on other side of road. 500m later, fork left downhill. Follow the track (clear, parallel to valley bottom, halfway up hillside) up and down hill, undulating above stream in valley below.

Itclimbs gradually.

Two km later take (upper) right track (village of Moldes visible high above to left on hillside). Continue uphill through chestnut woods. Track joins from back left. [RJ: keep straight on (left) downhill.] Keep straight on uphill to villageof Villasinde.

4km to **Villasinde**
Bar (not always open), fountain.
Directions:
Once again you have a choice, you can : a) continue to Herrerias (4km), or b) go down to Vega de Valcarce (2km, perhaps for a well deserved sleep).
If you opt for sleep, turn right along road on entering village. At bend by cemetery, fork right off road and turn left immediately down clear lane at side of road. This takes you (way marked) downhill into Vega de Valcarce. It turns left and left again, then right at the bottom to cross the Puente Viejo. Turn left on main road to rejoin main camino.
To continue to Herrerias: when you get to the road in Villasinde, cross, go up short street, turn left at top and go straight, passing left of church. Fork left at end, veer right and keep straight on (right) at fork uphill. Follow road for 1 km and keep straight on (right) at fork. (First TV antenna on left uphill).
Pass fountain on left after 1km. 500m later turn left downhill off very steep road 150m before a very large rock and red and white TV masts (500m after fountain). Continue down steep old track for 1 km, veering right near valley bottom. Turn right by bridge in Herrerias and left along road to rejoin main camino.

6km to **Vega de Valcarce**
(630m)
Pleasant village with adequate Pension Fernandez, (double room and breakfast 25 Euros). Bar and shops. First bar on right has good coffee. Refurbished refuge off Plaza Municipal has showers; charge of 1 Euros. Key at Bar Charli.

The Emperor Charles V dined and spent the night in this locality on 20 March 1520. On the way out of Vega de Valcarce, on a mountaintop on the left, you can see the ruins of the castle of Sarracin, dating from the fourteenth and fifteenth centuries. Its origins may go back to the tenth or eleventh. In its later period it belonged to the marquesses of Villafranca.

Opposite it, crowning the mountain that rises to your right, once stood the fortress known as Castro de Vega, but no traces of it remain.

Accommodation:
Refuge: (50) near Plaza Municipal. No kitchen and cold water. Bar Charly has the key and also good food. Pension Fernandez tel: 987 54 30 27. Double 30 Euros without bath. Single 18 Euros. Bar Manolo, 5 Euros. extra for shower.

Directions:
[After Vega de Valcarce the camino starts to climb, gently and later steeply, up to El Cebreiro. It continues, following the course of the river Valcarce. The river wends its way through chestnut woods, tiny villages and open country. It enters Galicia

at 1200m.]

Continue on the road to Ruitelan (bar/tabac). Just before road bends uphill to right, fork left downhill into Herrerias.

3km to **Herrerias** and HospitaI Ingles
(680m) (1336)

Village mainly oft the road down in the river valley and of interest to English pilgrims. The last houses of Herrerias were called Hospital in line with a papal bull of 1178 which mentioned a Hospital for the English. There was also a chapel in which pilgrims who had died were buried. At beginning of village on the old NV road is a bar. Down by river is a picnic place and bar nearby. Small shop.

Accommodation:

Paraiso del Bierzo has bar, menu and accommodation. A Casa do Ferreiro has menu and beds at 10 Euros. Food shop at crossing.

Directions:

Veer right over the river (the Dragonte variant rejoins the camino here from the left) and then road through village (bar, shop on left at other end).

(As the ground is often wet here many people in the village wear wooden clogs over their shoes in bad weather, each foot raised up off the ground on three "legs".)

At a "T" junction (signposted to the left to "San Julian 2") keep straight on (right). At the end of the houses there is a left turn marked "Lindoso2"; ignore this and keep straight on (right) here to "La Faba". Keep right on road and after crossing the second bridge go uphill for 1.5km. At two milestone-type marker posts (one for walkers, the other for cyclists, La Faba is visible ahead on clear day). Fork left down a foot path to the valley floor.

[If the weather is bad or very wet walkers are advised to continue on cyclist's route, a minor road with very little traffic, then a UMUR, going directly to Laguna de Castilla, missing out La Faba) to El Cebreiro –way marked and easy to follow.]

A clear rocky track zigzags its way steeply through chestnut woods to the village of La Faba.

4km to **La Faba**
(917m) (1340)
Bar (simple meals) summer only, church, 3 fountains.
Directions:
Fork left uphill at fountain. Continue through village, ignoring turnings to left and right. Keep straight on uphill at end. Fork right when lane comes out into the open. Go straight uphill along green lane to village of Laguna de Castilla.

2km to **Laguna de Castilla**
(1098m) (1342)
Directions:
Go straight through village, ignoring turns to left and right. Just outside the village you will observe the first of the Galician marker stones – it is 153km to Santiago from here. These stones, bearing the conch shell motif, are somewhat like old-fashioned milestones, placed at 500m intervals along the route. They fizzle out some 15km before Santiago. They are useful, telling the pilgrim the distance in kilometers to the next stop. They are also there to reassure you that you are not lost, particularly as the Camino now picks its way through a veritable maze of old lanes and tracks with constant changes of direction. The stones also tell you the names of the places you are in, very necessary, as many of the villages you will go through, are too small to have name boards.
Galicia is riddled with green lanes, none of which have signposts. These marker stones, obsolete though they might appear to be, are in fact very useful. In the province of La Coruna they are also used as way marks and have arrows indicating changes of direction.
Unlike Navarre and Castille–Leon, where the villages are bigger but widely separated, those in Galicia are often extremely small but very close to one another so you are not usually far from a building of some sort.
After 1km you will enter Galicia, in the province of Lugo (large

marker stone to right of camino). After 1km, past a wall with a wood above it (right) and a large stone barn (right) you will emerge onto the road at El Cebreiro.

GLACIA: The region's name says something about its history. Like Gales (Wales) and Gaul (France), "Galicia" indicates that the Celts established themselves here. Remains of their fortified villages survive intact. The "castros" are to be found everywhere in Galicia. Infiltration by the Romans was thorough and some of their excellent monuments, such as the walls of Lugo, still survive. From the fifth century on, the Suevi invaded the region, and shortly thereafter, the Visigoths. In 730 the Arabs tried to invade Galicia, without success. Against the prevailing military trend, it was the kingdom of Asturias which incorporated Galicia into its sphere of influence, until the Reconquista.

8km Cebreiro (1300m)
A tiny village of only 9 houses, a step back in time and one of the high points of the pilgrimage. The 12th c. church of Santa Maria contains relics and a 12th c. statue of the Virgin, which reputedly inclined its head after a miracle that took place early in the 16th century. Cebreiro developed from and for the pilgrimage and there was a hospital here from the 11th century until 1854, run initially by monks from the abbey of St Geraud of Aurillac in France. The village consists partly of 'pallozas', typical Galician thatched dwellings of Celtic origin, one of which is a small museum. Outside the church is a bronze bust of the late priest of Cebreiro, Don Elias Valina Sampedro, who devoted his life to Cebreiro and the practical and academic aspects of the pilgrimage. No shop as such (see below).

Accommodation:
The Hostel San Giraldo de Aurillac, next to the church is run by the family of the late Don Elias. It is not solely for pilgrims, has only 6 rooms and is often full in July and August. You are lucky if you find a room free. The cost is reasonable (40 Euros double) and the food good and substantial. The summer overflow

goes into the small house opposite. It is worth telephoning ahead on (982)-36.90.25 if you would like to stay there. Camping is possible in the field at the back. The hostel has a good selection of books and maps for sale.Meson Anton tel: 908 08 33 35. Double 45 Euros. Single 30 Euros. Meson Caloro. Double 40 Euros.

Refuge: large (68) new refuge opened in 1993, built by the Xunta (autonomous government) of Galicia. Facilities good but sleeping areas cramped. Two of the pallozas used in the past may be used for overflow pilgrims, but they have no water or light. Lady in the house next to refuge pallozas offers dinner and breakfast to pilgrims; bar on ground floor and dining-room on first floor.

3km to Linares
Accommodation:
Casa Jaime. Double 40 Euros. Meals, bar and shop.

3km to Hospital de Ia Condesa
A small village with beautiful, domed church and new refuge

(18) with showers and kitchen.

2km to Alto do Pojo or Puerta do Polo (1337m)
A huddle of houses, two of which are bars, with some accommodation: Meson El Polo has rooms, shop and pilgrim book. Posada del Peregrino is expensive and is not a refuge (in case you are told the refuge is full and are offered an expensive room). Cafe/bar Puerto has cheap rooms. Hostal /Rest Santa Maria de Poio tel: 982 36 71 67. rooms 35 Euros.

12km to Triacastela (665m)
Small village with a church dedicated to Santiago. Shops.
Accommodation:
Fonda Villasante, in modern building on right towards the end of the village. Hostel/Bar O'Novo very good but try to pay (and reclaim passport) the previous night if you want to make an early start. Meson Vilasante tel: 982 54 81 16. Double 40 Euros. Single 28 Euros. Bar Rio has meals, bocadillos and sello but has no rooms. Avoid the first restaurant on the left on main street. If you want breakfast at 7.30, go to El Peregrino opposite the refuge.

Refuge:
New refuge (60) with good facilities just outside the village. No bike storage. Overflow sleeps in church after 8pm Mass.

Directions
From Triacastela walkers have the choice of the road route to Sarria, via the monastery of Samos, or 18km along the old Camino via San Xil and Furela; good walking with fountains (no bars). Old Camino has excellent new refuge (22) some 10km after Triacastela and 8 before Sarria at Calvor. Own food needed.

10km to Samos
Large 17th c. Benedictine monastery with lengthy guided tours twice a day in summer.
Accommodation:

Refuge: (50) in monastery. Open at 1600. No kitchen. Hot bath. Hostal A Veiga tel:982 54 60 52. on road to Sarria. Double 50 Euros. Hostal Victoria is opposite refuge. Rooms 40 Euros. Breakfast at 6.30 AM. Rest. Resco andBar Espana have good menus.

12km (from Samos) to Sarria (420m)
A larger town and useful stopping place with banks and shops. The yellow arrows take you up the hill to the attractive old part. Romanesque church of San Salvador, 14th c. castle on the hill. Hotels are mostly in the lower, modern part of the town, to the right as you approach.

Accommodation:
Hostel Roma, calle Calvo Sotelo 2, is cheap and spacious (good double room for 30 Euros); no restaurant. Hostel Londres generally good value though rooms smaller. Good menu del dia' 7 Euros. Hospedaje Mar del Plata, near station has good double rooms (20 Euros). Cafe/bar Rivera at Vazquez Oueipo 19 has cheap, clean rooms (eg 10 Euros single). Bar El Faro and Bar Marseille also have rooms. The Fonda Burgalese, opposite the Hostal Roma, is not recommended unless you are stuck. Worth asking about rooms in the bars on the way up the hill in the old town. Taverna Lopez, rua Maior (in old town) and Restaurante/ Mesdn do Carreta both very good value for meals. Refuge: no refuge for individuals but the Padres Mercedarios up the hill in the old town has a refuge open only to large pre-booked groups.
Cycle Repairs: Pallares, calle Diego Pazos 46, tel. (982) 53.05.52.

4km to Barbadelo (580m)
A hamlet with fine Romanesque church dedicated to Santiago. Cyclists should turn off the Sarria-Portomarin road at km34 stone to the left, 2km out of Sarria, and follow rough but passable road through Vilel. Or carry on past church, turn right at next I junction and left at main road.Refuge: good new refuge (22)

in converted school. Kitchen.

Accommodation:
Refuge: (25) one km from village. Kitchen and hot baths. Casa Nueva de Rente. tel: 982 53 04 12. Double 40 Euros. Single 20 Euros. There is a bar selling tinned food and other basic things.

9km to Morgade
A hamlet with fountain, ruined chapel and a farmhouse which offers drinks and 'bocadillos'. Beds also available. Tel: 982 53 12 50.

1km to Ferreiros
A village with fountain and new refuge (22) with good facilities. 200 metres to Mirallos, a tiny hamlet with fine Romanesque

Accommodation:

Mesdn Rodriguez, calle Fraga Iribarne 6, has rooms and does a set meal; not cheap and quality and service variable. The Posada del Camino, centrally located by San Nicolas, is not recommended unless everywhere else is full. It is not to be confused with the Pousada de Portomarin, the town's luxury hotel, signposted near San Pedro.

Refuge (90) in former school, behind church is excellent with good facilities, hot showers, kitchen and drying area. 1 Euros charge. Opens around 3pm.

6km to Gonzar
A small village with church of Santa Maria and good new 1993 refuge (20).

6km to Ventas de Naron
Crossroads hamlet with useful Bar Novo, Hospital do Cruz, which does rooms and has 'sello'. New refuge (22).

4km to Ligonde
A village with some interesting houses. New small refuge; overflow may go into empty parish house.

1km to Eirexe (walkers only)
Detour to Vilar de Donas - some 15km after Portomarin and 1km after Eirexe at Portos (one house only) walkers and cyclists should try and make a small detour (2 1/2km for walkers, less for cyclists) to Vilar de Donas to see its fine Romanesque church of El Salvador (National Monument). It has paintings and impressive effigies of knights of the Order of Santiago who settled here in 1184. Their primary role, contrary to what you may read elsewhere, was not to protect pilgrims (although they did provide some hospitals for pilgrims) but to defend Christian Spain against the Moors.
Accommodation:
Refuge (20) Refugio de Ligonde. Kitchen and showers.

6km to Palas do Rei (565m)
A town with no features of special interest, although the neo-

Romanesque church has a good 11th c. west portal.

Accommodation:

Casa Curro at no.15 in first proper road to left. Avda de Orense, off main street as you enter town is recommended for both rooms and food. Bar Guntina is a fonda in the Travesia del Peregrino and does meals; clean and inexpensive, quality of meals variable and hot water uncertain. 500 metres out of town on the left is the Restaurante Pontarroxan: rooms and food good but not cheap. Refuge (49): in main street at the bottom of Travesia de Ia Iglesia was restored in1993 and reported good.

Detour for Cyclists - between Palas do Rei and Melide, cyclists who like castles will find a short detour to the Castillo de Pambre worthwhile. It is a fine well-preserved Galician castle, though inhabited by people who do not welcome visitors. Route is not well sign-posted in latter stages, so not a detour for those short of time.

5km to Mato

Walkers route only. New 1993 refuge (20).

3½km to Leboreiro

On walkers' route but close to road for cyclists. Village with simple, Romanesque church of Santa Maria and new (signposted on tree) refuge (30) with mattresses, kitchen (no pans) and showers. Water problems in the summer. Small bar/shop 500m back at road junction does good meals.

Accommodation:

Refuge (20) No beds and matresses. Kitchen and cold water. Near Coto is Casa de Somoza. Double 48 Euros. tel: 982 54 51 05. There are rooms at Bar/Resr. Zwei Deutches. Opposite house offers snacks and coffee.

6km to Melide (454m)

Important town with two Romanesque churches, San Pedro on the right at the entrance to the town and Santa Maria de Melide in the 'suburb' of Santa Maria on the western outskirts of the town. Key available nearby. The parish church in the town centre is Sancti Spiritus.

Accommodation:

Hostel/restaurante Estilo in town centre; rooms on expensive side for facilities but restaurant good. But it is impossible to leave until 9.30am. Hospedaje Xaneiro, rua San Pedro (close to main crossroads) has English-speaking proprietor, Maria, and is cheap and friendly. Bikes stored. Soly Mar restaurant is run by Maria's husband. Bodega Alongos, on left on main street as you enter town, has good, cheap food.

Refuge: very good, large (130) new refuge near the church of Santa Maria. Bunks, hot showers, kitchen, 'salon' and bike storage.

Note: between Castaneda (bar) and Ribadiso the camino crosses a new road. There is now a concrete 'bridge' which is passable by both walkers and cyclists.

12km to Ribadiso de Baixo

Has a good, new 1993 refuge (62). Cafe/Bar Manuel serves good food.

2km to Arzua (389m)

Pleasant small town, with church of Santiago and good shops.

Accommodation:

Fonda Frade is good, old-fashioned, family-run and cheap, double room 20 Euros; food copious. Hostel O'Retiro, just before the town and opposite a garage has acceptable rooms. Casa Teodora has rooms but reports vary; food acceptable. Fonda Carmen on main street has rooms in new flats down the road, but avoid its restaurant if possible.

Refuge: new refuge on western outskirts of town, reported small but good. Campsite: small, private Don Manuel campsite, only 200m from town centre (on left as you enter) and well signposted. Very pleasant class I site, with good facilities, including bar/restaurant and swimming pool. Open all year. Casa Frade, Rua de Ramon Franco, tel: 981 50 00 19. Double 45 Euros. Single 25 Euros. Hostal O`Retiro tel: 981 50 05 54. just before town. Double 50 Euros. without bath. Single 25 Euros. Food is cheap at Bar do Peregrino.

Cycle Repairs: Fidalgo, calle Santiago 12, tel.(981) 50.02.32.

Directions:

The route, on paths and the road, now passes through a number of tiny villages; several bars on or just off the route.

15km to Santa Irene

A new 1993 refuge, plus a private one, the Albergue de Peregrinos just up the road which costs 10 Euros a night and provides evening meal and breakfast. Good, cheap basic bar/restaurant on north side of road. (Are the private refuge and basic bar one and the same?)

2km to A Rua

Has useful Hostel Pino; double room 50 Euros and good menu at 9 Euros.

2km to Arca

Village set in eucalyptus forest. Shops and bars; the only one that does meals is opposite the Bar O'Muino up side road beside town hall. Refuge (80) is new for 1993 with good facilities including a washing machine and drier. It is probably located behind first pharmacy coming into village from the east on main road. Yellow arrows take the walker through eucalyptus wood to stadium; for refuge best to stay on the main road.

7km to Lavacolla

Now largely occupied by the airport of Santiago, it was the traditional washing place for pilgrims before they entered Santiago de Compostela. Now a place best avoided.

Accommodation:

Hostel La Concha has good food; rooms 40 Euros. but can be noisy. Hotel Garcas 2700 for single with bath and San Piao tel: 981 88 82 21. Rooms 54 Euros. Restaurants and bars are mainly expensive. Campsite: Monte del Gozo, with restaurant, pool and bar.

Note: the route from Lavacolla almost as far as Monte del Gozo is very badly way marked. It is tortuous as soon as one turns south off the main road, and particularly bad on the straight northern leg past the radio and TV station - don't turn back here. Adds several km to main road route.

5km to Monte del Gozo (Monxoi or Mount Joy) and chapel of San Marcos.

Celebrated as the first point from which the towers of the great Cathedral of Santiago could be seen and therefore a place of great joy for pilgrims. It was once a tranquil green hill. For 1993 the Xunta de Galicia erected a number of unsightly buildings on this historic site, including, on the right, 800 free refuge places for pilgrims; also an amphitheatre, campsite, roads, car-parking and restaurants.

Accommmodation:

The accommodation, though of a low standards, is reported comfortable and is useful for large groups and for anyone wanting to arrive in Santiago very early in the morning. There are eight hundred free places for pilgrims. The first night only is free. The site is crowned by an inappropriate modern monument. Individuals and small groups should have no trouble finding refuge or cheap accommodation in Santiago itself. Buses leave for Santiago every hour on the hour.

Directions:

From Monte del Gozo and San Marcos you can either take the quicker main road route or follow the longer, more peaceful alternative route (way marked) to the left round the south side of the hill to San Lazaro.

4km (or 7km) to San Lazaro (suburb of Santiago)

A chapel on site of former leper hospital.

SANTIAGO DE COMPOSTELA (264m)

Do not be too disappointed by the outskirts of Santiago, which are like those of most other Spanish towns of a similar size. The pilgrim way into the Cathedral after the chapel of San La zaro (just beyond the motorway) is via the following streets: calle de los Concheiros, rua de San Pedro, Cruz del Homo Sancto, Puerta del Camino, Casas Reales, PL. de Cervantes, calle Azabacheria, plaza de Ia Inmaculada and then either into the Cathedral by the Azabacheria (north) door, or straight on, down some steps and turn left into the main Plaza del Obradoiro to enter via the Portico de Ia Gloria.

If you cannot find the rua San Pedro, simply follow signs to the

Cathedral and the Plaza del Obradoiro, the monumental main square of Santiago, with the Cathedral, the Hotel de los Reyes Catdlicos (once a pilgrim hospital) and the 18th c. Town Hall with its long, classical facade.

At the main entrance to the Cathedral, climb the steps to the

famous sculpted portal of 1188, the Portico de Ia Gloria, and place your fingers in the worn Tree of Jesse under the statue of St James, a time-honoured pilgrim tradition.

The focal point of the Romanesque interior is the 13th c. statue of St James above the richly decorated high altar. Pilgrims can mount the stairs on either side to embrace the statue frombehind - another tradition known as 'a hug for the Apostle' - and descend under the altar to see the silver casket in which the remains of the saint are housed.

The giant censer, known as the Botafumeiro, will be swung less often than in 1993; on 25 July, St James's Day and other special days. Ask at the Pilgrim Office (see below) or the Tourist Office about when you can see it. Pilgrim Mass, if the 1993 tradition is followed, will be daily at 12 noon. The Holy Door in the Plaza de Quintana is closed until the next Holy Year.

Try and spend two or three days in Santiago as there is much to see and do. The numerous bookshops in the rua do Villar and elsewhere, e.g. Follas Novas, 1 calle Nueva (new town) stock guidebooks in English.

The Compostela - those who have walked or cycled the Camino and have their pilgrim records or 'credenciales' as proof of their journey should present themselves at the Pilgrim Office in order to btain the certificate of pilgrimage or 'compostela'. This

is situated in the fine Casa del Dean (1st floor) on the corner of rua do Villar and the Rua Gelmirez. Open 10 to 2 and also 5 to 7pm at busy times. Expect to be asked for the reasons why you made your pilgrimage as the Cathedral authorities want to ensure that 'compostelas' are not granted indiscriminately, for example to those travelling primarily as tourists. (See Confrater-nity Bulletin no.28, September 2000 for the views of the Cathedral on this subject.)

Once you have your compostela, you will be entitled to three free meals for three days at the magnificent Hotel de los Reyes Cadtdlicos, which maintains the tradition of pilgrim hospitality. However, these meals are served in the staff dining-room at unusually early hours for Spain, i.e. 9, 12 and 7pm. The food is filling but reports of its quality vary. There is a maximum of 10 pilgrims permitted at each meal. The hotel reception staff require a copy of your 'compostela' for each meal taken.

Get it photocopied at Sandine's at 23 rua do Villar and keep the original yourself. It may give free entrance to the Cathedral museums.

The Tourist Office (Oficina de Turismo) run by the Xunta de Galicia, is at 43 rua do Villar, one of three old and beautiful 18thc. streets behind the Cathedral. Its director, Don Jose Maria Ballesteros, speaks English and French and is an honorary member of the Confraternity. He will help with any problems, particularly over accommodation and the return journey. There may also be a municipal tourist office in a kiosk in the Plaza de Galicia, where the old town meets the new. The new Municipal tourist office is run by the Concello de Santiago. It is situated behind the cathedral in Rua do Vilar, beyond Hostal Suso.

Accommodation:

Refuge: (94) Seminario Menor de Belvis. Outside the old city centre. Open from 0630 to 2400. No kitchen. 5 Euros.

There is no shortage of other accommodation and prices vary. The tourist offices will have the full list of hotels. There are a number of cheap hotels near rhe bus station and in the streets leading from the cathedral to the new town, Rua Nova do Vilar. A few of the vast selection of hotels is given below:

Hostal Suso, Rua do Vilar 63 . tel: 981 58 11 59. Double 40 Euros. Bikes are accepted.

Hospedaje Santa Cruz, Rua do Vilar. single 25 Euros.

Hospedaje Noya, Rua do Vilar 13-1. Double 2500.

Hostal Barbantes, Rua de Franco 3 tel: 981 58 10 77. Double 55 Euros. Good cathedral view.

Hospedaje Lalin, Rua de Azabacheria 31. Double 30 Euros.

Hospedaje La Carballinesa, Patio de Madres 4. Double 35 Euros. A good friendly place. Bike storage.

Hostal La Estela, Avda Rajoy 1.tel: 981 58 27 96. Double 40 Euros. Very central. Off Plaza del Obradoiro.

Hostal Alameda, Rua de San Clemente 32. tel: 981 58 81 00. Double 75 Euros.

The Monastery of San Pelayo Antealtares, Plaza de Quintana. tel: 981 58 31 27. Limited accommodation.

The Residencias Maria Inmaculada, Rua Nova 8 is only for women.

Hogar San Francisco, near cathedral is expensive and central.

Hostal de los Reyes Catolicos. Plaza de Obradoiro. tel: 981 58 22 00 . Fifteenth centuary building. Good and expensive to stay. Bar serves drinks to non residents in the lounge. The hot chocolate and the grape juice are good. Food is disappointing.

Cycle Repairs: Vda Honorino, calle General Pardinas (in new town), tel. (981)

58.72.34.Rucksack Repairs: ask for Victoria Castro ('revetiadora') in the pharmacy in the Plaza San Miguel. Good and inexpensive.

Restaurants: A very wide variety, in all price ranges:

a) Cheap: El Asesino, Plaza Universidad 16; Meson Candilejas, Plaza Mazarelos; Casa Manolo, via Travesia; Los Cuatro Vientos, calle de Santa Cristina near San Roque. Also 9 rua del Fuente de San Miguel. Hot chocolate at Cafe Matate opposite entrance to monastery of San Pelayo is highly recommended.

b) Medium-priced: the Trinidad, calle de Trinidad; Tacita de Oro, 31 rua do Hdrreo, and a number of others in the calle del Franco.Estanco, 26 rua do Hdrreo does good paella. Rest./bar La Churrasquita, Plazuela de San Felix 6. Las Huertas, calle de las Huertas 16.c) expensive: gourmet pilgrims should head for the Restaurante Vilas, calle Rosalia de Castro 88, the Retablo, rua Nova 13 or Don Gaiferos, rua Nova 23.

Bars - Santiago is so full of bars that everyone will find their own favourite. Two interesting ones are the Cafe/Bar Derby, a traditional meeting place at the end of the old town, near the Plaza de Galicia, and the Bodega Abrigadoiro, calle Carrera del Conde 5 in the new town. The latter is a dark but respectable tavern with a working water-wheel that keeps the local white Ribeiro wine cool.

Places to Visit Outside Santiago - if you have time go to two pilgrim destinations beyond Santiago: Padron and Finisterre.

Padron: 20 km to the south and an easy train journey from Santiago railway station, if you don't feel like walking or cycling. Padro is where the boat bearing the body of St James after he was martyred in Jerusalem in AD44 is believed to have come ashore.

Known then as Iria Flavia, Padron today is a quiet country town. The parish church is down by the river and contains a large stone which is reputed to be the mooring stone of St James's boat. Approach the altar, open its doors and look down on a large stone with a strange inscription. The church is closed in the afternoon until around 5pm when a young man (who expects a tip) materialises with the key There is a pleasant walk up the hill behind the town where St James may have preached in the first century, after the death of Christ. Another place of interest in Padron, very near the station, is the museum of Rosalia de Castro, the renowned 19th century Galician poet. Padron has several bars, restaurants and hostels and makes a relaxed day out. Hostel Jardin (40 Euros double) recommended.

Finisterre: The end of the known world in medieval times and the final earthly destination for pilgrims. Today Finisterre, some 95km from Santiago, can be reached by bus from Santiago's bus station at San Cayetano. A bus leaves every morning at 7.45am, except Sundays, and goes direct to Finisterre (a ride of 2 to 3 hours). There is a return service in the evening but it is not direct and you will probably have to change at Vimianze. The lighthouse and the cliffs, the real 'end of the earth', are some 2½km further on from the village and are signposted.

Accommodation:

There are several hotels and fondas. The Hospedaje Lopez is clean, simple but modern, in the centre of the village, with a room costing around 16 Euros. The Casa Velay (rooms and meals) is highly recommended. The refuge, in the school near the port and across the street from the Post Office, now charges 10 Euros. If you do want to stay there ask for the person in charge (the 'encargada').

Spanish Language

Among all European languages, Spanish is closest to Portuguese and Italian. Spanish, has the simplest grammar of any Romance language, and if you know a little of any Romance language you will find much of the vocabulary here looks familiar. It's quite easy to pick up a working knowledge of Spanish. Spaniards will appreciate your efforts, and will correct you when you make mistakes, this is because they will be delighted you are trying to learn their language and will help you learn.

Spanish Pronunciation

Spanish pronunciation is phonetic but somewhat difficult for English speakers.

Vowels

- **A** short a as in 'pat'
- **e** short e as in 'set'
- **i** as e in 'be'
- **o** between long o of 'note' and short o of 'hot'
- **u** silent after q and gue- and gui; otherwise long u as in 'flute'
- **ü** w sound as in ''dwell''
- **y** at end of word or meaning, as i

Dipthongs

- **ai, ay** as in 'side'
- **ei, ey** as ey in 'they'
- **au** as ou in 'sound'
- **oi, oy** as oy of 'boy'

Consonants

c before the vowels i and e, it's a castellano tradition to pronounce it as th; many Spaniards and all Latin Americans pronounce it in this case as an sch like ch in 'church'

d	often becomes *th*, or is almost silent, at end of word
g	before *i* or *e*, pronounced as j *(see below)*
h	silent
j	the chin loch—a guttural, throat-clearing *h*
ll	**y** or **ly** as in million
ñ	*ny* as in canyon (the ~ is called a tilde)
q	*k*
r	usually rolled, which takes practice
v	often pronounced as *b*
z	*th*, but **s** in parts of Andalucia

Stress is on the penultimate syllable if the word ends In a vowel, an *n* or an *s*, and on the last syllable if the word ends In any other consonant; exceptions are marked with an accent.

Useful Words and Phrases

yes	*sí*	please	*por favor*
no	*no*	thank you (very much)	*(muchas) gracias*
I don't know	*No sé*	**you're welcome**	*de nada*
I don't understand	*No entiendo*	**It doesn't matter**	*No importa*
Spanish	*español*		
Do you speak English?	*¿Habla usted ingles?*	**excuse me**	*perdóneme*
Speak slowly	*Hable despaclo*	**Be careful!**	*Tenga cuidado*
Can you help me?	*¿puede usted ayudarme?*	**maybe**	*quizá(s)*
		nothing	*nada*
Help!	*Socorro*	**It is urgent!**	*Es urgente*
How do you do?	*Cómo esta usted?*	**How ...?**	*¿Cómo...?*
or more familiarly	*¿Cómo estas?*	**How much?**	*¿Cuánto/Cuánta?*
	¿Qué tal?	**How many?**	*¿Cuántos/Cuántas?*
Well, and you?	*¿Bien, y usted?*	**I am lost**	*Me ne perdido*
or more familiarly	*¿Bien, y tú?*	**I am hungry**	*Tengo hambre*
What is your name?	*¿Cómo se llama?*	**I am thirsty**	*Tengo sed*
or more familiarly	*¿Cómo te llamas?*	**I am sorry**	*Lo siento*
My name is...	*Me llamo.../ Mi nombre es...*	**I am tired**	*Estoy cansado-a*
		I am sleepy	*Tengo sueño*
Hello	*Hola*	**I am ill**	*No siento bien*
Goodbye	*Adios/Hasta luego*	**Leave me alone**	*Déjeme en paz*
Good morning	*Buenos dias*	**good**	*bueno/buena*

Good afternoon	*Buenas tardes*	bad	*malo/mala*
Good evening	*Buenas noches*	slow	*despaclo*
What is that?	*¿Qué es eso?*	fast	*rápido/rápida*
What...?	*¿Qué…?*	big	*grande*
Who	*¿Quién...?*	small	*pequeño-pequeña*
Where...?	*¿Dónde...?*	hot	*caliente*
When	*¿Cuándo...?*	cold	*frío fría*
Why...?	*¿Por qué...?*		

Directions

I want to go to...	*Deseo ir a...*	there	*allí*
How can I get to...	*¿Cómo puedo Ilegar a...?*	close	*cerca*
		far	*lelos*
Where is... ?	*¿Dónde está... ?*	left	*izquierda*
When is the next...?	*¿Cuándo sale el próximo..?.*	right	*derecha*
		st~.aight ~	*todo recto*
What time does it leave (arrive)?	*¿Parte (llega) a qué hora?*	forwards	*adelante*
		backwards	*hacia atrás*
From where does it leave?	*¿De dónde sale?*	up	*arriba*
Do you stop at...?	*¿Para en... ?*	down	*abajo*
How long does the trip take?	*¿Cuánto tiempo dura el idaje?*	north (n./adb)	*norte/septentrional*
		south (n./adj.)	*sur/meridional*
I want a (return) ticket to...	*Quiero un billete (de ida y vuelta) a..*	east (n./adj.)	*este/oriental*
		west (n./adj.)	*oeste/occidental*
How much is the fare?	*¿Cuánto el billete?*	corner	*esquina*
Have a good trip!	*Buen viaje*	square	*plaza*
here	*aquí*	street	*calle*

Numbers

one	*uno/una*	twenty one	*veintiuno*
two	*dos*	thirty	*treinta*
three	*tres*	thirty one	*treinta y uno*
four	*cuatro*	forty	*cuarenta*
five	*cinco*	forty one	*cuarenta y uno*
six	*seis*	fifty	*cincuenta*
seven	*siete*	sixty	*sesenta*
eight	*ocho*	seventy	*setenta*
nine	*nueve*	eighty	*ochenta*
ten	*diez*	ninety	*noventa*
eleven	*once*	one hundred	*cien*

twelve	*doce*	one hundred and one	*ciento-uno*
thirteen	*trece*	five hundred	*quinientos*
fourteen	*catorce*	one thousand	*mil*
fifteen	*quince*	first	*primero*
sixteen	*dieciséis*	second	*segundo*
seventeen	*diecisiete*	third	*tercero*
eighteen	*dieciocho*	fourth	*cuarto*
nineteen	*diecinueve*	fifth	*quinto*
twenty	*veinte*	tenth	*décimo*

Time

What time is it?	*¿Qué hora es?*	morning	*mañana*
It is 2 o'clock	*Son las dos*	afternoon	*tarde*
half past 2	*...las dos y media*	evening	*noche*
a quarter past 2	*...las dos y cuarto*	today	*hoy*
a quarter to 3	*...las tres menos cuarto*	yesterday	*ayer*
		soon	*pronto*
noon	*mediodia*	tomorrow	*mañana*
midnight	*medianoche*	now	*ahora*
month	*mes*	later	*después*
week	*semana*	it is early	*está temprano*
day	*dia*	it is late	*está tarde*

Shopping and Sightseeing

I would like...	*Quisiera...*	money	*dinero*
Where is/are...?	*¿Dónde está/están...?*	museum	*museo*
How much is it?	*¿Cuánto vale eso?*	theatre	*teatro*
open	*abierto*	newspaper	*periódico*
dosed	*cerrado*	pharmacy	*farmacia*
cheap/expensive	*barato/caro*	police station	*comisari'a*
bank	*banco*	policeman	*policia*
beach	*playa*	post office	*correos*
booking/box office	*taquilla*	postage stamp	*sello*
church	*iglesia*	sea	*mar*
hospital	*hospital*	shop	*tienda*
Do you have any change?	*¿Tiene cambio?*	supermarket	*supermercado*
		tollet/tollets	*seivicios/aseos*
telephone	*teléfono*	men	*señores/hombres/caballeros*
telephone call	*conferencia*		
tobacco shop	*el estanco*	women	*señoras/damas*

Days

Monday	*lunes*	**Friday**	*viemes*
Tuesday	*martes*	**Saturday**	*sábado*
Wednesday	*miércoles*	**Sunday**	*domingo*
Thursday	*jueves*		

Months

January	*enero*	**July**	*lullo*
February	*febrero*	**August**	*ago sto*
March	*marzo*	**September**	*septiembre*
April	*abril*	**October**	*octubre*
May	*mayo*	**November**	*noviembre*
June	*junto*	**December**	*diciembre*

Accommodation

Where is the hotel? *grande*	*¿Dónde está el hotel?*	**with 2 beds**	*con dos camas*
		with a double bed	*con una cama*
Do you have a room?	*¿ Tiene usted una habitación?*	**with a shower/bath**	*con ducha/baño*
Can I look at the	*¿Podría ver la*	**for one person!**	*para una per sona!*
room?	*habitación?*	**two people**	*dos personas*
How much is the room per day! week?	*¿Cuánto cuesta Ia habitación por dial semana?*	**for one** night/ **one week**	*una noche una semana*

Transport

aeroplane	*avión*	**platform**	*andén*
airport	*aeropuerto*	**port**	*puerto*
bus/coach	*autobtis/autocar*	**seat**	*asiento*
bus/railway station	*estación*	**ship**	*buque/barco*
bus stop	*parada*		*embarcadero*
car/automobile	*coche*	**ticket**	*billete*
customs	*aduana*	**train**	*tren*

Restaurant

menu	*carta/mentú*	**Can I see the menu, please?**	*Dém el menú por favor*
bill/check	*cuenta*		
change	*cambio*	**Do you have a wine list?**	*¿Hay una lista de vinos?*
set meal	*menú del dia*		
waiter/waitress	*camarero/a*	**Can I have the bill (check), please?**	*La cuenta, por favor*
Do you have a table? for one/two?	*¿Tne una mesa? ¿.. para uno/dos?*	**Can I pay by credit card?**	*¿Puedo pagar con tarjeta de crédito?*

Spanish words used in the guide

Ajimez	in Moorish architecture, an arched double window
Alameda	a park or promenade
Ambulatory	semicircular aisle around the high altar of a church
Artesonado	*mudêjar-style* carved wooden ceilings
Atalaya	Phoenician word for tower*Ayuntamiento* city hail
Azulejo	painted glazed tiles, popular in Moorish and *mudêjar-work* and later architecture
Baldachin	canopy on posts over an altar or throne
Barrio	city quarter or neighbourhood
Bóveda	vault
Calvarlo	calvary, or outdoor Stations of the Cross
Caprna Mayor	seat of the high altar in a cathedral
Cartuja	a Carthusian monastery
Caserlo	Basque country house or chalet
Castizo	anything essentially Spanish (from the Castilian point of view)
Castro	Celtic or Iberian fortress settiement
Castrum	Roman military camp
Churrigueresque	florid Baroque style of the late 17th and early 18th centuries in the style of Joni Churriguera (1650—1725), Spanish architect and sculptor
Ciudadela	a citadel
Converso	Jew who converted to Christianity
Coro	the walled-in choir in the centre of a Spanish cathedral
Corregidor	royal magistrate
Cortes	Parliament
Cromlech	circular ring of stones
Diputaciòn	seat of provincial government
Embalse	reservoir
Ermita	hermitage
Fueros	exemptions, or privileges of a town or region under medieval Spanish law
Granja	farm or farmhouse
Hidalgo	literally 'son of somebody'—the lowest level of the nobility, just good enough for a coat-of-arms
Homage tower	the tallest tower of a fortification, sometimes detached

	from the wall
Hórreo	Asturian or Galician granary or corn crib
Isabelline Gothic	late 15th-century style, roughiy corresponding to the English perpendicular
Juderia	Jewish quarter
Mirador	a scenic overlook or belvedere
Modernista	Catalan Art Nouveau
Morisco	Muslims who submitted to Christianization to remain in Spain after the Reconquista
Mozaráb	Christians under Muslim rule in Moorish Spain
Mudéjar	Moorish-influenced architecture; Spain's 'National style' in the 12th—16th centuries
Ogival	pointed (arches)
Pallazo	circular, conical-roofed shepherd's hut in Asturias and Galicia
Patio	central courtyard of a house or public building
Pazo	Gallcian manor house
Plateresque	16th-century style; heavily ornamented Gothic
Plaza	a town square
Plaza de Toros	bullring
Plaza Mayor	square at the centre of many Spanish cities, often totally enclosed and arcaded
Posada	inn
Pronunciamiento	a military coup
Puerta	gate or portal
Reja	iron grilles, either decorative ones in churches or those covering the exterior windows of buildings
Retablo	carved or painted altarpiece
	Sala Capitular chapterhouse
Transitional	in northern Spanish churches, referring to the transition between Romanesque and Gothic

Some statistics on the pilgrimage to Santiago

The number of people undertaking the pilgrimage to Santiago as recorded by the Cathedral authorites in Santiago.

1986	2,491	
1987	2,905	
1988	3,501	
1989 (Pope's visit)		5,760
1990	4,918	
1991	7,274	
1992	9,764	
1993 (Holy Year)		99,439
1994	15,863	
1995	19,821	
1996	23,218	
1997	25,179	
1998	30,126	
1999 (Holy Year)		154,613
2000 (Jubilee Year)		55,004

Roughly 70% of pilgrims each year are men, 30% women; 70% make the journey on foot, 30% by bike (though in 2000 the proportion was closer to 80:20) . The statistics for 2000 (possibly still untypical, though not a Holy Year) show that 44% of pilgrims were under 30; 36% were between 31 and 50. The percentage of those over 50 has grown from 16% in 1997

PILGRIM ASSOCIATIONS

FRANCE

Paris: 4 Square du Pont de Sevres, 92100 Boulogne-sur-Seine

Aquitaine: Clos des Obiers, 33170 Gradignan Malatic

BELGIUM

Flemish: sint-Andriesabdij-Zevenkerken, 8200 Brugge 2

French: rue de Marbais, 7, 6320 Viller-La Ville

NETHERLANDS

Leeuwerikwide 2. 3742 XR Baam

GERMANY

Aachen: H.K. Bahnen, Wilhelmstr. 50-52, 5100 Aachen

Dusseldorf: H. Wippper, Ziegeleisweg, 89, D-4000 Dusseldorf.

Köln: H. Simon, Melanchmonstr. , 24, D-500 Köln 80.

ITALY

Via di Verzaro 49, 06100 Perugia

SWITZERLAND

Lignon, 43, ch-1219 Geneve.

SPAIN

Aragon: Casa de la Cultura, C/Levante, 22700 Jaca

C/Bellido 17, 22700 Jaca

Paseo Cuellar 10, 56006 Zaragoza, Tel: 275280.

Navarre: Sierra de alaiz 5-8°C, 31006 Pamplona Ttel: 240975

Garcia el Restaurador, 6-7°, 31200 Estella. Tel: 551429

La Rioja: Menendez Pelayo, 10-6°C, 26004 Logroño Tel. 243261

Apartado 60, 26250 Santo Domingo de la Calzada (Revista Peregrino / Peregine Magazine) Tel: 350134.

Castile Leon: General Yagüe, 6-7°C 09004 Burgos Tel: 20547.

Ayuntamiento, Plaza de San Telmo, 34440 Fromista

Monasterio MM. Benedictinas, 24320 Sahagun

Rua, 33-1B, 24003 Leon. Tel: 252796

Colegiata de San Isidoro, 24003 Leon. Tel: 236600

C/La Granja, 37, 24390 Dehesas-Ponferrada.

Galicia: Avenida da Coruña, 313-6°b, 27003 Lugo

Santiago Cathedral. Tel: 562419 & 562578

La Rosa, 20-4°, 15701 Santiago Tel: 592521

Laxe, 11-61D, 36202 Vigo

Asturias: General Elorza, 60-4°C, 33001 Oviedo

Madrid: San Amaro 1, 28020 Madrid Tel: 2706382

Catalonia: Numancia 107-109, 08029 Barcelona

Valencia: Arzobispo Fabian y Fuero 24-1°, 46009 Valencia

Basque Counry: Dr. Camino 5-6°, 20004 San Sebastian. Tel: 429745

Getting to Roncesvalles from Pampolona

Public transportation is available by bus or by taxi.

BUS to Roncesvalles
Previously known as 'La Montañesa', now 'Autocares Artieda'
 +34 948 330 581
Monday – Friday: 18:00
Saturday: 16:00
Sundays: No service
Price: € 3.91

TAXIs to Roncesvalles
Asociación TeleTaxi and Asociación Radio Taxi are two local agencies.
+34 948 232 300, +34 948 230 000, +34 948 232 100, +34 948 221 212
+34 948 220 971, +34 948 351 335, +34 948 221 144

WEEKDAYS TAXI TO THE FOLLOWING

(Weekend Rates are slightly more)

Pamplona - Roncesvalles € 42.00

Pamplona - Valcarlos € 54.00

Pamplona - Saint Jean de Pied de Port € 68.00

Pamplona - Puente La Reina € 21.00

Pamplona - Estella € 37.00

Pamplona - Los Arcos € 52.00

Pamplona - Torres del Río € 59.00

Pamplona - Viana € 68.00

Index

A
Alto de Erro 39
Alto del Perdon 52
Alto de Mezquiriz 37
Alto de San Anton 82
Alto do Pojo or Puerta do Polo 198
Antonines french order 117
Antonio Mengs painter 117
Anunciada Franciscan convent 177
Apeadero Villamarco 134
Arab aesthetic school 106
Arab invasions 140
Arabs 75
Arca 205
Archaeological Museum Cacabelos 174
Arles 15
A Rua 205
Arzua 204
Astorga 157
Atapuerca 99
Augustin 13
Augustobirga roman town 113
Ayegui/Irache 65
Aymeric Picaud 143
Azofra 86
Azqueta 67

B
Baroque 81
Basilica de Nuestra Senora de la Encina 169
Basilica de San Isidoro pilgrim church 143
Basque 32
Belorado 93
Benedictine monastery 114
Bercianos del Real Camino 136
Bernard Montaner 63
Bishop Miguel Sanchez de Uncastillo 47
Boadilla del Camino 121
Botafumeiro giant censer 201
Braga 11
Burgos 103
Burgos cathedral 104
Burguete 36

C
Cacabelos 173
Calzada del Coto 133
Calzadilla de la Cueva 129
Calzadilla de los Hermanos 134
CAMINO REAL FRANCES 135
Camping: 22
Campo 168
Camponaraya 173
Capilla del Condestable 106
Cardenuela 100
Carlos III 46
Carrion de los Condes 126
Casa del Angulo doorway 108
Casa de Miranda palace 108
Castanares 102
Castildelgado 92
Castillian School of Art 107
Castrojeriz 117
Cathedral Museum Astorga 157
Celtic 10
Chapel of Virgen del Camino 47
Charlemagne 32 126
Charles V Emperor 186
Chozos de Abajo 153
Church of San Cernin 47
Cirauqui 58
Cizur Menor 50
Cluniac 131
Cluniac Order 12
Cluny 1283
Coimbra 11
Columbrianos 172
Counts of Lemos 169
Cruz de Ferro 164
Cueza river 128

D
Dominican 148
Dona Blanca of Castile 84
Dona Mencia de Mendoza 98
Dragonte 189
Druids 10

E
Edward III 110
Eirexe 201
El Acebo 164
EL Burgo Ranero 137
El Cid 126
El Cid tomb 105
El Ganso 161
Enrique II 111
Episcopal see Astorga 156
Ernest Hemingway 45
Esla river 139
Espinal 37
Espinosa del Camino 94
Estella 61

F
Fernando III 105 115
Fernando II of Leon 169
Fernando IV 115
Ferreiros 200
Finisterre 10
Finisterre lighthouse 206
Flemish 157
Foncebadon 163
Franciscan 131
Franciscans 85
Francisco de Colonia 105
Francisco de Miranda canon 108
French immigrants at Villafranca 175
Fresno del Camino 152
Friar Martin Sarmiento writer 177
Fromista 122
Fuentesnuevas 173

G
Gaudi Antonio 158
Gonzalo de Berceo pilgrim 87
Gonzar 201
Gothic cathedral 46
Grand Abbot of Cologne 34
Granon 91

H
Herod Agripa 11
Herrerias 193
Holy See 98
Holy Sepulcher 12
Hornillos 116
Hornillos del Camino 115
Hospital Ingles 193
Hospital de la Condesa 198
Hospital de Orbigo 154
Hospital of San Anton 117
Hospital of San Miguel 47

I
Ibaneta 33
inares 198
Ira Flavia 11
Isabel I of Castile 99
Italian influence 122
Itero de la Vega 121

J
Jacobean monuments 76
Jacobean motifs 85
Jewish synagogue 64
Jews 91
John the Baptist sculpture 135
Juan II 111

K
Koenig german pilgrim 83

L
La Faba 195
Laguna de Castilla 195
Language: 18
La Peregrina monastery 131
La Rioja 75
Larrasoana 41
Las Huelgas Abbess 110
La Sociedad Bar 53
La Trinidad church 131
Lavacolla 206
la voje ladee 10
Leboreiro 203
Ledigos 129
Leon 141
Le Puy 15
Ligonde 201
Linzoain 38
Logrono 75
Lorca 59
Los Arcos 70

M
Madres Benedictinas convent 132
Madres Bernardas monastery 90
Maneru 56
Manjarin 164
Mansilia de las Mulas 138
Mansilia de las Mulas (799m) (1178,317) 138
Maps and Guidebooks 16
Mary Magdalene 64
Mato 203
Melide 204
menhirs 10
Milky Way 52
Mohammed 6
Molinaseca 167
Monte del Gozo 206
Moorish arches 170
Moors 1275144153
Moral de Valcarce 189
Morgade 200
Moslem invasion 6
Murias de Rechivaldo 161
Muruzabal 53

N
Najera 83
Navarrete 81
Nuestra Senora de Belen 127
Nuestra Senora de Belen hermitage 93

O
Obanos 53
Oncina del la Valdoncina 152
one*See also* none

Opening and closing times: 24
Orbaneja 100
Orbigo river 153
Order of the Holy Sepulchre 71
Ordono II 140

P
Padron
Pamplona 44
Pedro I 111
Pelagius, 11
Peroja river 96
Planning the Day: 24
Planning Your Journey 15
Plaza del Castillo 44
Plaza del Obradoiro Santiago 201
Poblacion de Campos 124
Pompey 44
Ponferrada 169
Ponte de Arga 54
Pope Pius VI 117
Portomarin 200
Preparing for the Journey 17
Procession of Santo Domingo's bread 77
Provincial Archaeological Museum Burgos 108
Provincial Archaeological Museum Leon 145
Puente la Reina 54
Puente Villarente 140
Puerta de la Pellejeria 105
Puerto del Romero Burgos 108
Puerto del Sarmental 105

Q

R
Rabanal del Camino 162
Rabe de las Calzadas 114
Ramirez I 75
Redecilla del Camino 91
Refuges 21
Reliegos 138
Returning from Santiago - 25
Ribadiso de Baixo 204
Riego de Ambros 165
Rioja Alta 75
River Ulla 11
River Ulzama 43
Road safety: 23
Rocamador monastery 64
Roland battling Farragut 67
Romanesque art Leon 143

Romanesque bridge 55
Romanesque Christ Pantocrator 62
Romanesque doorway 51
Roman road, Via Trajana 133
Roncesvalles 33
Ronzabal 33
Route Napoleon 30

S
Sahagun 131
Saint-Jean-Pied-de Port 2829
Salado river 59
Salfonso XI 115
Samos 199
Samos Benedictine monastery 192
San Adrain monastery 138
San Andreas church 170
San Andres Benedictine monastery 174
San Felix de Oca monastery 95
San Fernando cloister 111
San Fiz de Seo 191
San Francisco church Villafranca 176
San Francisco monastery 93
San Juan Bautista church 63
San Juan De Ortega 97
San Juan de Ortega 97
San Justo de La Vega 156
San Lesmes tomb 107
San Martin del Camino 151
San Miguel del Camino 150
San Miguel hermitage 124
San Milan de Cogilla monastery 88
San Nicolas church 107
San Nicolas Jesuit monastery 177
San Pedro Romanesque church 197
Sansol 70
Santa Ana church Leon 141
Santa Catalina de Somoza 161
Santa Clara (XIII century) convent 126
Santa Clara convent 63

Santa Maria church 73
Santa Maria church gothic 59
Santa Maria de Carbajal convent 141
Santa Maria del Castillo gothic church 122
Santa Maria del Manzano church 117
Santa Maria del Palacio church 77
Santa Maria in Belorado church 93
Santa Maria la Blanca 125
Santiago airport 199
Santiago el Real church 77
Santiago Matamoros 6
Santibanez de Valdeiglesias 156
Santo Cristo of Burgos 107
Santo Domingo de La Calzada 88
Santo Domingo monastery 62
Santo Domingo tomb 89
Santo Tomas de las Ollas church 170
San Zoilo monastery 127
Security: 23
Song of Roland 32
St. Francis of Assisi 12
St Denis 114
St John of Jerusalem 50
Suso is Visigoth monastery 87

T
Tardalos 114
Templar's Castle 169
Templars village of 125
Teobaldo II 62
Terradillos de los Templarios 129
The devil 52
Theodomir, bishop
Torres Del Rio 71
Tosantos 94
Tourist Office Santiago 203
Trabadelo 182
Triacastela 198
Trinidad de Arre 43

U
Urbanizacion de Santiago 150
Urbiola 69
Uterga 52

V
Valcarlos 31
Valdearcos river 137
Valverde de la Virgen 150
Vega de Valcarce 192
Venta del Caminante 39
Venta del Puerto 39
Ventas de Naron 201
Vezelay 15
Viana 72
Villabilla de Burgos 113
Villadangos del Paramo 151
Villafranca del Bierzo 175
Villafranca Montes de Oca 95
Villafria 101
Villalcazar de Sirga 125
Villa mayor 68
Villamayor Del Rio 92
Villar de Corrales 190
Villar de Mazarife 153
Villares de Orbigo 155
Villasinde 191
Villatuerta 60
Villava 43
Villavante 153
Villavieco. 125
Virgen de la Majestad cathedral 157
Virgen del Camino 148
Viscarret 38
Visigoths 153

W
white cock and hen legend 89

X

Y

Z
Zabaldica 42
Zariegui 51
Zubiri 40
Zuriain 42

To users of this Guide:

Whilst every effort has been made to check the accuracy of the information contained in this Guide, the publishers can take no responsibility for errors or omissions. Users are invited to report on these, and their experience to the publisher.

We wish to thank the numerous pilgrims who made the pilgrimage who have offered practical advice and helped to keep this guide accurate.

www.ingramcontent.com/pod-product-compliance
Ingram Content Group UK Ltd.
Pitfield, Milton Keynes, MK11 3LW, UK
UKHW041430180426
11947UKWH00007B/367